The Rivalry:
How Two Schools Started the Most Played College Football Series

By Chuck Burton

Edited by Kim DePaul

DEDICATION

To Kim and Eric, who are with me today because of a chance meeting at a football game in Princeton, and whose love and support inspired me every day to finish this book.

To my Grandma and Grandpa Hankel, who met during a college football practice.

To my Mom, and Dad, who always go to homecoming at Dartmouth, even in the rain and snow.

To my Nana and Grandfather Burton, who are reading this in Heaven.

To my extended family members who play or appreciate college football.

And especially to my Great-Uncle Jimmy, who blew his college savings to fly in a plane to see his school, Washington and Lee, play in a football game. This has to be where I get my love of football.

CONTENTS

ACKNOWLEDGMENTS

I would like to thank the sports information directors and archivists at Lehigh University and Lafayette College for their help over the years, especially Phil LaBella at Lafayette, and Steve Lomangino at Lehigh. I'd also like to thank Lehigh's Athletic Director Joe Sterrett, and Lafayette's Athletic Director Bruce McCutcheon for their help and support.

This book couldn't have been written without the archives of *The Brown and White* and *The Lafayette* newspapers, and the school departments responsible for making them available online 24/7. It also couldn't have been written without *The Morning Call* and *The New York Times* archives, and other newspapers too numerous to count.

A special thanks to the University of Pennsylvania's archives department; David Coulson of the College Sports Journal; Ava Bretzik, director and historian of the Asa Packer Mansion Museum; Margaret Whitehead, curator of the Blithewold Mansion, Gardens & Arboretum; The Library of Congress; the Internet Archive (home for a treasure trove of public domain documents); and Google (which has an impressive amount of their own public domain information from this era). Without all of these amazing tools, and helpful people, this book would not have been possible.

FOREWORD

My first exposure to the football program at either Lehigh or Lafayette came on Nov. 28, 1998.

I was the 22-year-old assistant director of communications at the Atlantic 10 Conference on that day, hired out of college to be the league's football sports information director, or SID, and rather lamentably for my 22-year-old self, to perform other duties like staff the indoor track and field championship and write the league's field hockey notes. (What a punk. I should have been happy I had a job).

But my main gig was football, and so it was that I sat in the University of Richmond's press box as the A-10 rep, watching the Spiders -- our league champ -- face Lehigh in the first round of the I-AA playoffs. I spent much of the game considering my travel plans for the following week, when Richmond -- the heavily-favored No. 3 seed, playing a lightly regarded No. 14 seed from the Patriot League on this warm Saturday -- would undoubtedly move on to play UMass or McNeese State in the quarterfinals.

I frankly didn't expect much from the team wearing brown. Lehigh was new to the playoffs, and the Patriot League -- from the still somewhat misunderstood world of 'non-scholarship football' -- was relatively new to the postseason as well. The Patriot's champion (Colgate) had been blown out by our champion (Villanova) in the first round the year before. I pored over my hotel choices for next weekend.

As it happened, I would end up in Amherst, Mass. on the first Saturday in December, which was good news for the league (UMass was in the A-10 too). What wasn't good news for the league? The team wearing brown would be there too.

Lehigh had stunned Richmond, 24-23, behind the right arm of the most impressive quarterback I'd seen that year in our league or any other, a guy named Phil Stambaugh. He looked like a pro in leading a last-second drive toward a game-winning field goal, which was rather fitting since he would eventually be a pro. The win was of critical significance for the Lehigh program, and for the Patriot League, which proved it belonged in the conversation on the national level of I-AA. There was an awakening that day, and I was one of those awoken.

When I gave up the field hockey notes about 18 months later and began working as a I-AA (later renamed the Football Championship Subdivision, or FCS) columnist for *The Sports Network*, which covered that group of Division I football programs and ran its Top 25 poll, major awards and All-America team, what I'd learned about the Patriot League on that Thanksgiving weekend in Richmond proved rather instructive. This was a quality league full of tremendous rivalries -- none bigger than the Lehigh/Lafayette game held every November.

The FCS level is often heralded for the purity of its game. Though not without its politics, it's the highest level of football to remain largely unspoiled by the corrupting influences that come with unimaginable wealth. The endgame for FCS programs and the universities that field them is not millions in playoff payouts or TV contracts, and the endgame for players at the FCS level is generally not to reach the NFL and become millionaires (though it does happen somewhat regularly). While an oversimplification, the FCS is more or less football for football's sake, but remains a high-quality brand of the game.

And with that purity comes some very pure, very real, very intense rivalries, none greater than Lehigh/Lafayette. College football's most played rivalry is pure because the hatred *is* pure. My tenure covering FCS football at *The Sports Network* happened to coincide with a period when Lehigh was up, under the great head coach Pete Lembo, and Lafayette was rebuilding its program under the equally classy Frank Tavani. I heard from a great many Lehigh fans during that period (most of whom wanted me to not use the alumni-detested nickname of "Mountain Hawks"), and the glee over their superiority to that school 20 minutes or so away shined through like a beacon in much of our correspondence.

When the Leopards upset the Mountain Hawks (sorry, Lehigh alums) on the last day of 2002, helping to deny Lehigh a playoff berth, my email inbox overflowed with notes from the formerly seldom-heard voices of Lafayette supporters. It was like a communist regime had been overthrown, and Leopards fans were no longer bound by the constrictions of state-run media. By the time Lafayette won in Bethlehem in 2007, to make it four straight wins in the series, I had moved on to covering the NFL. I can only imagine what my email box might have looked like that day.

In the forthcoming pages, Chuck Burton has laid out in detail the many twists and turns of the early rivalry, illustrating (sometimes literally) what has made the rivalry great. I'm so glad this book exists -- the uninitiated need to understand.

And if you need any further evidence of the meaning of Lehigh/Lafayette, I'll leave it to the aforementioned Phil Stambaugh, who was so impressive on that November day in Richmond. He would go on to graduate Lehigh with school records of 10,575 passing yards and 78 touchdown passes. He'd lead his team to the I-AA playoffs twice and would ring up all-conference and All-America honors. He'd make money in the NFL, NFL Europe and the Arena League. And yet he remains unwavering about his finest achievement as an athlete.

"Nothing stands out for me more than being 4-0 against Lafayette," Stambaugh told the Express-Times in 2013. "That's what I'm most proud of. I don't have any love lost for them at all."

- Tony Moss
  General Editor, ESPN Insider (College Basketball)

1. BEGINNINGS OF A CONFLICT

One of the main ingredients of a great Rivalry in any sport involves a deep-seated conflict between two close regions or groups of people.

For example, when Celtic plays Rangers in the Scottish Premier League in soccer, both clubs are separated by religion (Catholic vs. Protestant), politics (Labor vs. Conservative), and historic proximity.

Barcelona and Real Madrid are not just separated by the fact that their soccer teams are the best in Spain, their rivalry is also defined by Barcelona historically representing the Catalonian separatist movement, and Real Madrid representing the Franco-led dictatorship that kept Madrid in control of what Barca fans might call Catalonia.

When Michigan plays Ohio State in football, a true border dispute, the "Toledo War," has been mentioned as a historic reason why the people of Michigan have always had some level of dislike for the folks from Ohio.

Lehigh and Lafayette, who have faced off on the football field more than any other two schools, have all of this, too.

Before the English came to colonize America, the Lenni Lenape Native American tribe (also known as the Turtle Clan) controlled the area of land that is now called the Lehigh Valley.

Like many other Native Americans, the Lenape were nomadic people, migrating to different places over a large area of land. Some of the areas that would become a part of Easton and Bethlehem were traditional hunting, fishing, and foraging grounds for the Lenape.

By the late 1600s the Five Nations Alliance of Native American tribes, led by the Iroquois Nation, considered the Lenape a part of their dominion.

The Pennsylvania Lenape territory was not in dispute until 1681, when William Penn, the Quaker founder of Pennsylvania, was granted a large parcel of land in America from King Charles II of England.

Penn named his new land or nation "Sylvania," which in Latin means "forest land," to which the King added "Penn" to the name in honor of his father William, an admiral and war hero for the British.

The Hon. William Penn, c. 1718

Penn's vision for his new nation was to be based on the emigration of the English Quaker population.

He wanted his people to be governed by his revolutionary ideals of freedom of worship, trial by jury, and free elections. Strict non-violence was a central tenet of his new colony. He also made it clear that he was a friend to the native peoples that already lived in his area, the Lenape.

"I am very sensible of the unkindness and injustice that has been too much exercised towards you by the people of these parts of the world," Penn wrote to the Lenape population from England, "who have sought themselves, and to make great advantages by you, rather than be examples of goodness unto you. I am not such a man, as is well known in my own country. I have great love and regard toward you, and I desire to win and gain your love and friendship by a kind, just, and peaceable life."

In 1682, only a year after the land grant from the King, Penn struck a treaty with the Lenape, paying Tamamend, the leader of the Lenape at that time, for use of their lands.

At a famous public meeting with William Penn, Tamamend stated that the Lenape and the English settlers would "live in peace as long as the waters run in the rivers and creeks and as long as the stars and moon endure."

But despite Tamamend's bold proclamation and Penn's high ideals, tensions between the Delaware Indians and the new English population remained strained.

Penn's religious ideals of peace and freedom were not only popular with the Lenape, who had more rights in Pennsylvania than they did in other states, but it also made Pennsylvania very popular with immigrant people escaping religious persecution, with waves of settlers pushing increasingly further north into the Lenape territory. The area saw English, German and Dutch settlers, of all different religious denominations, increasingly at odds with one another.

As Pennsylvania's colony expanded in the early 18th century, the Penn estate in England would fall into ruin. William Penn was sent to debtor's prison in England after his financial advisor had effectively embezzled huge chunks of his estate, nearly forcing Pennsylvania to be sold back to the English crown. William Penn died penniless in 1718, and his sons Thomas and John were deemed the proprietors of the Pennsylvania colony, land-rich and cash-poor.

The Penn sons, by all accounts, had a different agenda than their Quaker father.

Almost immediately after being assigned charge of Pennsylvania, the Penn brothers went about selling large chunks of land to English real estate speculators like William Allen and James Logan, even though the English had no legal claim to much of this land from the Lenape.

This is when the Rivalry between the peoples of Bethlehem and Easton began.

Mural of Walking Purchase, Hotel Bethlehem

After a series of such claims, in 1737, the initial land for what would eventually become Bethlehem and Easton was officially acquired from the Lenape Indians by what would infamously be called the "Walking Purchase," or "Walking Treaty."

Whether through desperation, guile or both, John and Thomas Penn claimed a treaty was made in 1680 between the Lenape and their father. The text of the treaty allegedly stated that "land to be deeded to the Penns was as much as could be covered in a day-and-a-half's walk."

3

The deed was incomplete and unsigned. At best, it was a contract that was never consummated. At worst it was a forgery.

"We see above that great emphasis is laid upon a Deed which is said to have been granted over fifty-five years before, the so-called Deed of 1686," an official English investigation noted in 1759. "Yet, though it is mentioned here as lying on the table, and although the Indian speaker says he had seen it with his own eyes, yet it is still questionable as to whether there really was such a Deed. It is certain that no such Deed is in existence now. Nor has it ever been recorded. Instead they produced a writing, said to be a copy of that Deed but not attested nor even signed by anyone as a true copy."

"THE POINT" AS IT APPEARED MORE THAN HALF A CENTURY AGO.

Easton, 1700's, Condit's History of Easton

English landowners, among them William Allen and James Logan, had already signed deeds to lands in that area, and stood to profit handsomely once the land officially became a part of the new country called Pennsylvania. The pressures on the Penns were enormous to deliver the land, so the Penns in turn pressured the Lenape.

Finally the Lenape were coerced into agreeing to the terms of the "contract," allowing the Proprietaries, as the group of landowners were then known, as much land as could be claimed after a "day and a half's walk."

"Three expert walkers had been obtained," the reverend Uzal W. Condit noted in his book *The History of Easton*, by which he meant the fastest runners in the county. "The trees had been 'blazed' [over the course of two years] in the preliminary walk, so that there need be no time lost in hunting paths," he continued. "The place of starting was fixed at a large chestnut tree, where the road from Pennsville meets the Durham road, near the Wrightstown meeting-house."

One of those "walkers" was Edward Marshall, the man whose "walk" would be the basis for the Proprietaries' land grab.

The walkers took off at sun-up running northwest of Wrightstown, with men on horseback in tow to carry them food and to minimize any need for the "walkers" to stop.

It was the Penns who planned out the route, making the path as easy to travel as possible - a path that ran northwest instead of north, as the original document allegedly stated, in order to claim more land.

After a day and a half "walking," Marshall made it all the way up to an area that would ultimately be named the town of Mauch Chunk.

Then, from the point where Marshall stopped, rather than draw a line due east to the Delaware River to delineate the new territory, they instead drew a line perpendicular to their walking path - northeast - back towards the Delaware River.

It didn't quite double the amount of land claimed by the English, but it came close - resulting in an area claimed for the landowners that was almost the size of Rhode Island.

"The walkers crossed the Lehigh [River] at Jones' Island," Condit said in *History of Easton*, "a mile below Bethlehem, and passed the Blue Mountain at Smith's Gap in Moore Township, Northampton County."

The Penn brothers and their soon-to-be-rich early land investors would waste no time in converting the land into money and prestige for the new colony. They would also unwittingly planting the seeds for future tensions.

They and their Proprietary friends started off by setting aside 1,000 acres of land at a strategic point next to the Delaware River for a town to be called Easton, named after the estate of the English family whose daughter Thomas Penn had recently married, Ms. Juliana Fermor.

Her father, Lord Pomfret, lived in Easton Neston House in Towcester, Northhamptonshire, in England, and Thomas chose the prime territory of the Walking Purchase, the convergence of the Lehigh and Delaware rivers, to place it.

The Penns and their associates also quickly made Easton the central hub of commerce, law, and activity for the entire region. Since Easton was situated at the forks of three rivers, it was a prime area called the "Forks of the Delaware." The word "forks" was applied to local names and landmarks.

They would base one particular name of a strategic river on one of those Lenape names, "Lechauwiechicuk," which meant "where there are forks." The name of this river would ultimately be shortened to "Lehigh" to describe the river which flows through the area west of Easton.

Bethlehem would be founded on the banks of the "Lechauwiechicuk" only a short time later.

A group of Moravian settlers, a remnant from a larger colony in Georgia, purchased a 500 acre tract of land from William Allen along the banks of the Monocacy Creek near the Lehigh River, only three years after the "Walking Purchase" occurred.

The leaders of this mission community, David Nitschmann and Count Nicholas von Zinzendorf, named their settlement Bethlehem, founded on Christmas Eve of 1741.

Painting of Count Nicholas von Zinzendorf, Germany

It was also founded on an area the Lenape coveted in terms of its abundant wildlife for hunting and fishing. "The historian of the Moravians tells us that the Indians would catch two thousand shad in a single day at Bethlehem," Condit notes in his *History of Easton*, "and at the junction of the rivers their efforts would be equally successful. This scene in its wildness was the capitol of the noble Delaware Tribe."

That was also a vital reason the banks of the Monocacy Creek were chosen as the site for the new Moravian settlement.

Missionary work with the Lenape was a central part of the Moravians' worldview, doing God's work to convert the Lenape and other Native American peoples to Christianity. Believing the Native Americans were a lost tribe of Israel, they felt it was their moral duty to convert them, with von Zinzendorf an active member in interacting with the Lenape.

The Comenius Foundation website says about von Zinzendorf, "as far as we have been able to identify, he is the only European noble to have gone out to meet the Native American leaders in this manner."

Bethlehem Settlement, 1700s, History of the Lehigh Valley

A nearby settlement called Gnadenhütten was set up, whose purpose was to allow the Lenape to find Christianity and live a Christian life. Like the Presbyterians, Lutherans, and German Reformed churches that had set up shop in Easton, the Moravians were Protestants. All were in the competition for Native American souls.

But the Moravians were the most successful at this venture, and they ran their settlement much differently than Easton - or any 18th century town.

The Church owned all the real estate and the flock was separated into "choirs," separated by age and sex, and driven by a strict culture of Church worship.

The goal of the Moravians was to live their interpretation of the earliest Christians of Jerusalem. That is how their communal system of operation - called "the economy" - was set up, where members performed manual labor for the good of the colony. "All that the members of this association gave was their time and the work of their hands," Bishop E. De Schweinitz's *Moravian History of Bethlehem* mentioned. "In return they received the necessaries of life and the comforts of home."

Another natural resource - the intersection of the creek and the Lehigh

River - helped the Moravians to design the first water pumping system of the English colonies in America, something that amazed Benjamin Franklin and John Adams during their mid and late 18th Century visits. Both had never seen such an invention.

Though Adams and Franklin didn't approve of the entire lifestyle of the settlers, their different, communal and religious way of living was something they both noted in their private journals on their visits to Bethlehem.

Between 1742 and 1746, about six hundred new "well educated and enlightened Moravians" settled in the Bethlehem area, according to *History of the Lehigh Valley*. "Such an occurrence has not taken place in any other of the United States, and the effect produced by six hundred intelligent persons, dropping, as it were, from the clouds into a region of darkness... may well be imagined. This 'light set upon a hill,' shedding abroad its refulgent rays, spread terror into the minds of those who came within its piercing effects. Their deformity, heretofore obscured, became visible, and, consequently, this light was simultaneously attacked from every quarter. The German and the Irish population of the county, who had always met at daggers' points before, were in this case united in deprecating the intrusion. Both the Irish and the Germans, in their quarrels among themselves, after having exhausted their vocabulary of expletives, in describing a bad man, to cap the climax, were wont to add that such a one was as bad as a 'd — d [sic] Herrnhutter.'"

"Herrnhutter" would be a derogatory term commonly used against the Moravians, and concepts like free schooling for children, and the education of Native Americans and girls were seen as a threat to the way of life as defined in Easton. Nevertheless, the Moravians conducted their business, despite "continuing very frequently under implications and threats."

In 1752, the Moravians in Bethlehem and the people of Easton would add political differences to go along with their tribal differences.

The land-owning Proprietaries, many of whom lived and worked in Easton, were led on the board of trustees by William Smith, the then-president of the University of Pennsylvania. He established Easton as the new county seat of government, at least in part to make Easton into the business center of the area as well as a religious and educational center.

In doing so, they were acknowledging that they were in direct competition with the Moravians in Bethlehem for both commerce and regional power. After all, there could only be one business center, and the Proprietaries wanted to make sure that it would be Easton, not Bethlehem.

The record shows that the Proprietaries made many conscious actions to keep the Moravians of Bethlehem less prosperous and more isolated - and thus remain second to Easton.

One such element of rivalry involved a key barren tract of land separating Bethlehem from Easton called the Dry Lands.

While known at that time for having very few resources available for food and water, it also happened to house the only road from Bethlehem to Easton, an old Lenape path called the King's Path, or Minisink Path. "From time immemorial, [the Lenape] passed to and fro [on the path], between the Blue Mountain and the Tide Water," according to Condit's *History of Easton*.

Travelling on this road required lots of supplies and careful planning. In the cold of winter or heat of summer, traversing the road by horse or by foot was treacherous due to the lack of "huts" along the route providing food and water.

Count von Zinzendorf got involved in an effort to help out his settlement.

"It would be no more than right for the Proprietaries to make us a present of the ground over which it passes," he wrote to one of the Moravian brethren on March 15th 1743, "because usually all the roads are given gratis, and because the width of this one is of no account to the Proprietaries, the country through which it passes being absolutely a desert without wood or water, and of such a nature that it never can be sold."

But the Proprietaries were not only unwilling to accommodate von Zinzendorf - there's evidence that they were actively working against him.

"To the westward and northward of the Dry Land, are the Moravian settlements, about eleven miles from the town," William Parsons, one of the Proprietaries, wrote to fellow landowner Richard Peters in England on December 8th, 1752. "These settlements are not only of no advantage, but rather a great disadvantage to the town... and as their number is continually increasing by the yearly addition of foreigners, it is not likely that they will, in time to come, raise sufficient provisions for themselves, but are obliged to purchase great quantities from their neighbors, who would otherwise bring it to the town; but this is not to be expected while they can dispose of what they have to sell so much nearer home [in Bethlehem]; and this leads me to wish, for the good of Easton, if the Honorable the Proprietaries should incline to have the Dry Lands improved, that it may not be disposed of to the Moravians. Not because they are Moravians, but because their interests interfere so much with the interests of the town."

This nine year interference in Bethlehem's emergence as a settlement was evident too in delays and foot-dragging in approving critical roads being built - not only to link key areas of need for the townspeople, but also to prevent a major thoroughfare from being developed from the bustling city of Philadelphia directly to Bethlehem.

"It must be borne in mind that the *granting* of a road was an entirely distinct affair from the *building* thereof," Condit's *History of Easton* mentioned, "and in almost every case, years elapsed between these two operations, as, for instance, the road of the Macungie German settlements, to the Lehigh [River] at Bethlehem, which was laid out in 1745, was no more than a bridal [sic] path for at least fifteen years, and it was considerably after 1760 before it became, in any sense, a wagon road."

Another hardship to get to and from Easton was a variety of taxes that fell disproportionately on the Moravian settlement.

Lehigh River, 1700s, History of the Lehigh Valley

"A tax was assessed on single men, of nine shillings each," *History of Easton* continued, which hit the Moravians, and their single-sex communal system with lots of single men, more than the farmers and families in the surrounding areas.

Furthermore, if the German settlers in Bethlehem had any grievances, Easton was also set up as the seat of county government and the only polling place in the county. Any court or county business would require a dangerous trip along the undeveloped Minisink Path, and when they got there, the official language of business was English, a language that the great majority of Moravians did not speak.

"The remote situation of Easton is grievous, and greatly expensive to all," stated a protest petition from May 15th, 1765, "but in a more particular manner to jurymen, widows, and orphan children, whose attendance is indispensably necessary, and who must travel with great danger and expense to the said town, that it frequently happens that persons who are summoned by the sheriff to attend at the courts on grand and petit juries do neglect or refuse to give their attendance on account of the great distance and expense, to the hindrance and delay of the public service; that the petitioners, moreover, are out to much greater charge per mileage, payable to the sheriff on all suits, by reason of the remoteness of the said town, to their great impoverishment."

Even though Count von Zinzendorf attempted to buy a portion of the otherwise-worthless Dry Lands at a price much more than their worth in order to improve the road, the Proprietaries declined to sell it to them - which undoubtedly contributed to the Germans and Moravians aligning themselves to the political party that had started to oppose the Proprietaries, the Quaker Party, backed by Benjamin Franklin and the Quakers in Philadelphia.

In fact, the rivalry between Bethlehem and Easton made them pawns in the political battles in Philadelphia between Benjamin Franklin and the Penn brothers, who greatly disliked each other.

One of Franklin's goals with the Quaker Party, or "anti-Proprietor party" as it was also known, was to change the nature of the Penns' proprietorship of all of Pennsylvania, which would have affected the Eastonians greatly.

The "Friends," as they were known, did much to convince the Moravians, and the other German immigrants of the area, that they should vote for the Quaker party - including resorting to propaganda to meet their ends.

"A... pamphlet supposed to have been written by Samuel Wharton in 1765," Matthew Schopp Henry writes in his book *History of the Lehigh Valley*, "says that the Quakers, [by means of German newspaper publisher C.]. Sower] persuaded the Germans that there was a design to enslave them, to compel their young men, by a contemplated militia law, to become soldiers, and to load them down with taxes. For this cause, he adds, they come down in shoals to vote, carrying everything before them."

The bitter political feud would pit both townships against one another for a time, but two larger conflicts would quickly unite both peoples against a common enemy: marauding Indians and the French/Indian War.

Teedyuskung, the newest leader of the Lenape, used the outrage of the Walking Purchase to rally many people to his cause. He pointed to the Walking Purchase as the ultimate proof that the Western settlers were only motivated for themselves and not the Lenape, and that they would continue to cheat to steal away the lands of his people.

Aligning themselves against the English, troops loyal to Teedyuskung initiated a savage attack against Gnadenhütten, slaughtering the converted Indian population and causing the pacifist Moravians to bear arms.

It was in the aftermath of these attacks that Benjamin Franklin himself made his first visit to the Moravian settlement in Bethlehem to supervise the creation of a system of forts to protect the city, something that couldn't have made the Proprietaries in Easton very happy.

Additionally, members of Ben Franklin's political party were meeting with Teedyuskung secretly in order to find a peaceful settlement for the Lenape. They wanted to come to a resolution on the unjust (in their view) acquisition of the Lenape land – and, in the process, discredit the Proprietaries.

The Quaker Party would ultimately get their way, negotiating an end to the Lenape's involvement in the French/Indian War through their workings with Teddyuskung. It would end with the Treaty of Easton, ironically cementing Easton's status as the political center of the region.

The negotiated end of the war with the Lenape would be signed in Easton, but the aftermath of that peace would be a lingering rivalry between the people of Easton and Bethlehem.

2. TWO SIMILAR PLACES

The ingredients of a great sports Rivalry involve, at some level, similarity. The rivals can see themselves in the other team to some degree. In the best case scenario, their histories are intertwined, consisting of the same cast of characters.

Harvard and Yale share a deep, intertwined history, and are similar institutions of higher learning, as are Maine and New Hampshire, Holy Cross and Boston College, Army and Navy, and many others.

The Yankees and Red Sox have a great and storied rivalry because sometimes the best players on their teams have played for both sides - the most well-known of those men being Babe Ruth.

In Lehigh and Lafayette's case, they are not only very similar in terms of academics and worldview, but their rivalry goes one step further. These schools were also, indirectly, founded by the same man.

The Moravians believed in the revolutionary concept that education for all was to be an instrument of salvation - for every human being, boys and girls, rich and poor.

Once Bethlehem's settlement started to thrive, setting up a school was a top priority as a part of their religious mission.

Less than a year after the Bethlehem settlement was founded in 1741, Countess Beningna von Zinzendorf, the daughter of Count Nicholas von

Zinzendorf, was a driving force behind the foundation of the Bethlehem Female Seminary, the first female boarding school in the Colonies.

Along with two boys schools founded a year after the Female Seminary, construction on all the schools was finished during the height of the tensions between the Proprietaries and the Moravians.

There is also evidence that Easton's first attempt at educating its youth may have been spurred on by the Moravians' new schools.

Bethlehem Female Seminary, History of the Lehigh Valley

In a letter from Proprietor Thomas Penn to England dated February 25, 1750, one of the founders of Easton wrote of the political clout of the residents of Bethlehem: "I am greatly alarmed to find the Germans behave so insolently at the elections; they must no doubt do so from the numbers given them at the back counties (which included Bethlehem, among others). The taking of counties from Bucks and Philadelphia (Easton's county Northampton, and nearby Berks) will take off their settlements, and leave them only two members of eight, and prevent them for many years from having a majority."

Samuel Wharton, one of Penn's collaborators and first cousin of Tom Wharton, Jr., the first president of the University of Pennsylvania, expressed his opinion about this electoral result as well.

"Wharton imputes their [voting preference] to their 'stubborn genius and ignorance'" Henry opines in *History of the Lehigh Valley*, "which he proposes to soften by education. To this end he proposes that faithful Protestant ministers and schoolmasters should be supported among them; that their children should be taught the English tongue... and to incline them sooner to become English in education and feeling, should compel them to make all bonds and other legal writings in English, and that no newspaper or almanac should be circulated among them unless also accompanied by the English thereof."

While the Moravians are not mentioned by name, the implication of this letter, and the timing, shows that the Proprietaries were very interested in assimilating the new German immigrants to their way of doing business - as opposed to the Moravians.

A little more than a decade after the Bethlehem Female Seminary was founded, the citizens of Easton built a small schoolhouse with the expressed purpose of "educating poor Germans." Through donations by a multitude of royal donors, it was completed in 1755.

"Rev. Schlatter, a German Reformed Church minister, exerted himself greatly in behalf of the Germans, and the formation of the society owed its origin to his exertions," Condit's *History of Easton* stated. "A large number of the nobility in England contributed liberally. King George the Second subscribed one thousand pounds, the Princess of Wales one hundred pounds, etc. etc. The funds thus created were distributed by trustees appointed. William Smith, then-president of the University of Pennsylvania, being one of the trustees, subscribed thirty pounds towards the building of the school-house at Easton."

Unusual for the time, the board of trustees at the school was set up to consist of multiple denominations. Condit noted that "five ministers of the German Reformed, and five ministers of the Lutheran denominations" were on its board of trustees, even though the day-to-day teaching and running of the school was done by Presbyterians.

It is no coincidence that the Rev. Michael Schlatter was chosen for this endeavor, and it was no coincidence that the denominations listed in the board of trustees involved five members of the German Reformed Church.

The German Reformed Church and Moravian Church were very much at odds with each other in the Lehigh Valley, with Schlatter's frequent collaborator, the reverend John Phillip Boehm, and the founder of the Bethlehem settlement, Count von Zinzendorf, in competition for souls and dueling over doctrine.

Lafayette College was founded in 1824, two score and seven years after the Declaration of Independence was signed in Philadelphia.

In many ways, though, Lafayette's founding was the culmination of decades of focus on the growing English and American value of education.

"The whole people must take upon themselves the education of the whole people and be willing to bear the expenses of it," then-president John Adams said in an oft-quoted letter to a foreign correspondent in 1785. "There should not be a district of one mile square, without a school in it, not founded by a charitable individual, but maintained at the expense of the people themselves."

(By the time John Adams wrote his letter, the "Moravian Young Ladies Seminary" had a tremendous reputation in early America as one of the few places where women could receive a quality education. The daughters and nieces of George Washington, Ben Franklin, Ethan Allen, and Adams were students there.)

Similarly, the upper class citizens of Easton started to think it important not only to "educate" its wealthiest residents but all of its townspeople – a revolutionary concept that was sweeping the young nation.

The schoolhouse built in Easton in 1755 was effectively expanded in 1794 to become the Easton Union Academy, a boarding and day school.

The intent of the academy was to model it after some of the oldest British-themed grammar schools in early America, like Hopkins Day School in New Haven and Boston Latin School in Boston.

Like Bethlehem's women's seminary, Easton Union Academy was also nationally known.

Rev. John Vanderveer

The principal was Mr. Andrew Mein, a Presbyterian minister who conducted religious services in English for the Easton Religious Society, which would ultimately form the First Presbyterian Church of Easton.

But Easton Union's biggest claim to fame was its English teacher.

The Presbyterian Rev. John Vanderveer, who had graduated from Princeton at the young age of 17, started out as an assistant at Easton Union and quickly became a well-known teacher in the community. Under his tutelage Easton Union rapidly grew into an academy of several hundred students with a reputation for English education.

Vanderveer was known for strict discipline, a highly desired trait among educators at that time.

"He was always master of the situation," Condit's *History of Easton* said. "He was quite severe with the birch; and, as an old pupil remarks, 'he could do this well.'"

Vanderveer ran a tight ship, which is why the school was so successful.

"The success which attended his efforts made his school the most remarkable centre of educational influence in Northeastern Pennsylvania," Condit continued. "While the school was busy, a loud rap upon the desk would be heard, followed by the order 'Face to the North,' and instantly books were laid aside, and all wheeled into position to listen to words quite as wise as those of the old Grecian teacher."

"That another cause of his success was his absolute independence," an old pupil told Condit. "He could say to his pupils, 'If you don't like the arrangements here, there is the door; you are under no obligations to attend this school. I care not to whom related, or whom begot, if you don't want to learn, and if you are unwilling to obey directions, leave at once.'"

Easton Union's national reputation was secured when Secretary of State Thomas Pickering, shortly after being dismissed by President John Adams in 1800, would relocate his family so that his son, John, could study under Vanderveer.

It is said by those at Boston Latin that Harvard University was created to educate those that graduated from there - after all, Boston Latin predates Harvard in age by several years.

The same can be said for Easton Union Academy.

"There are but few young men in and around Easton, that have not attended the excellent boarding and day school of the Rev. John Vanderveer, which for many years was considered the stepping-stone to the Lafayette College," Matthew Shopp-Henry's *History of the Lehigh Valley* noted.

It can be argued that Lafayette College was created to expand the educational opportunities for the recent graduates of Easton Union - and would, additionally, allow Easton to one-up the Moravians in Bethlehem in terms of being a "center of education" once and for all.

"Local communities created academies that grew into colleges, and various churches endeavored to assure the propagation of their sects at the intellectual level by establishing denominational colleges," Albert Gendebein stated in *The Origins of the Pardee Scientific Course at Lafayette College*. "This spirit, transforming collegiate education from an almost exclusive class institution into a bulwark of the nation, was the motivating force behind the hopes and actions of Easton's citizens. Only one of the charter trustees of Lafayette College was a college graduate, Joel Jones of Yale College and the Litchfield Law School. All the rest wanted for their sons something that had not been thought necessary or even desirable by their fathers."

Even though the charter trustees had not received formal education, however, didn't mean they didn't know, or care, about education.

Eastonian James Madison Porter was born on November 6th, 1793, the youngest child of the Revolutionary War hero Andrew Porter.

His father, who started out as headmaster of a mathematics school in Philadelphia before duty called, rose quickly in military service to colonel of the Fourth Regiment of Artillery. "Colonel Porter was personally engaged in the battles of Trenton, Princeton, Brandywine, and Germantown," *The History of Easton* said, "and when the siege of Yorktown was determined upon, he, at the special personal request of the Commander in Chief [Gen. Washington], took charge of the laboratory at Philadelphia for the preparation of the ammunition necessary for the use of the army."

James Madison Porter

The wealthy, educated Colonel Porter was a teetotaler, a military expert and a political force, occupying the appointed positions of surveyor general of Pennsylvania. He also declined several plum jobs over his life, including the positions of chair of mathematics by the University of Pennsylvania and secretary of war by President James Madison. His career would be defined by military service, commitment to education, and the temperance movement.

His legacy would loom large in his sons' lives.

Colonel Porter's sons, James, George, David and Robert, would dominate politics in the early 19th century, partially due to their father's influence and contacts.

George would be appointed the first governor of the Michigan Territory in 1831; David would end up being a renowned, Democratic governor of Pennsylvania in 1838; Robert would become a powerful, long-serving judge in nearby Berks County; and James would found a large, extremely lucrative law practice in Easton. (In addition, one of his half-sisters, Eliza Ann Parker, would be the mother of a future first lady, Mary Todd Lincoln.)

It was in this environment, in his father's surveyor general's office, that James Porter, at the young age of sixteen, became a clerk. There he worked alongside his older brother Robert, learning the intricacies of law and politics.

His background of law and education, along with time in his father's office, made him an expert in something that would be very valuable in the

Lehigh Valley during that time frame.

The surveyor general worked with the Pennsylvania Land Office by recording and forwarding warrants for private land claims, which, in the early part of the 19th century, involved the beginning of extremely lucrative business interests.

For this purpose the office had some of the most detailed maps of the area. An intelligent young man clerking in this office would have a very good idea where natural resources might lie - and could, with some money and some good contacts, make himself a wealthy man as a result.

Shortly after being appointed attorney general for all of Northampton County, he would marry his wife (Eliza) in 1821, and then use his formidable powers of political persuasion only three years later to help found Lafayette College.

Without correspondence or letters, it is difficult to ascertain why James Madison Porter wished to found an institution of higher learning. There are plenty of hints, however, in his biography and family history that provide insight.

"To the Honorable Senate and House of Representatives of the Commonwealth of Pennsylvania in General Assembly met," the official charter, presented to the Legislature of Pennsylvania, declared. "The petition of the subscribers, inhabitants of the said Commonwealth, respectfully represents. That a memorial has been presented to your honorable bodies on behalf of the Trustees of 'Lafayette College,' located in Easton, praying for an act of incorporation. Your petitioners, believing that the plan of education proposed to be adopted in that institution, in which military science and tactics will be combined with the usual course of academical studies, and a due attention paid to the modern languages, especially the German, will be productive of much good to the students and the public in general; and that such an institution is much needed in this section of the State, pray your honorable bodies that a charter of incorporation may be granted to the said Trustees, and such Legislative aid be extended to the funds of the institution as you in your wisdom may deem proper."

Lafayette was not founded with the principle of being a purely liberal arts school, though it was influenced by the classic liberal arts schools of the time. It was not founded with the idea of being strictly a military college, though it was influenced by certain military academies. It was not meant to be solely a religious school, though it was meant to be taught and run by Presbyterians.

It was a hybrid of both scholarly pursuit and military tactics, with religious instruction as well. In short, it was a college to reflect well-rounded students of the classic languages - including, notably, the English language, likely pulling from the strengths of Easton Union Academy - and the values in education that had served James Madison Porter's and his father's careers very well.

Porter himself did not attend a college or university, though some of his brothers did. He did, however, attend Norristown Academy and had a scholastic environment at home, considering his father's background as a headmaster in Philadelphia.

It was his father's military link that caused Lafayette College to be named after the famous Revolutionary War hero, the Marquis de Lafayette.

In 1824, there was a great nostalgia for the heroes of the Revolutionary War, not only in Easton and Bethlehem but all around the young nation.

While George Washington had already passed away, former Presidents John Adams and Thomas Jefferson were still alive, but were in their twilight years, unable to travel. The French hero of the Revolution, the Marquis de Lafayette, embarked on a farewell tour around the former colonies, widely assumed to be his final tour of the land he helped liberate from English oppression.

It's no surprise that the Marquis was a superstar in America in his twilight years. As a key member of the Revolution, he fought with Washington at the battles of Monmouth and Yorktown, and was an American hero of the same caliber as the other American founding fathers - a still-living link to the founding of the country.

With its peculiar demography, Easton was one of the first towns of the Revolution with a Committee of Safety to protect its citizens, predating similar ones in surrounding areas such as Newark and Philadelphia. This committee would end up being the operating government of the early Colonies.

From this provisional government came the first draft of soldiers to protect the new nation, and many male members of Easton, Bethlehem, and surrounding areas were members of the fighting force. Some fought at Valley Forge, others took part in the Flying Camp of reservists in the main phase of the Revolutionary War, and still others took part in Sullivan's Expedition, where the Continental Army marched to New York to defeat the English's new allies, the Iroquois, and cement victory for the Revolution.

Eastonians were proud of their links to the Revolution, and may have felt the need to wave their flag a little higher than their neighbors to the west in Bethlehem, where, by decree of General Washington himself, the General Hospital of the Army was relocated in 1776 from Morristown to move it further from the line of battle.

The Marquis convalesced in Bethlehem for a month after the Battle of Brandywine to recuperate from injuries. Originally, during his farewell tour, he had planned to visit there.

"Since this step could not be included in the trip," David Bishop

Skillman wrote in his book, *The Biography of a College*, "Easton determined to honor the aged hero by sending her various military organizations to the reception in Philadelphia."

A group of 200 Eastonians, including Porter and Jacob Wagener (another Lafayette founder and son of a soldier who fought with the Marquis), marched away on Wednesday morning, Sept. 22, 1824, to see General Lafayette one last time in person.

"Two days were spent floating and rowing down the Delaware in Durham boats to Philadelphia and two days walking back," *The Biography of a College* said. "Six days were occupied in the stirring scenes connected with the welcome to the fine, old Frenchman."

They would make it down the Delaware River to Philadelphia to see their hero.

"On hearing his name," *The Biography of a College* continued, Lafayette then said, "Porter, Porter, I remember that name. Any relation to Capt. Porter, whom I met at Brandywine?"

"Yes, sir, a son," replied Porter.

"Well, sir," said the general, "I bless you for your father's sake. He was a brave man. He had with him there a young man, a relative I think whose name I have forgotten. They fought very nearly together."

"Was it Parker?" asked Mr. Porter.

Marquis de Lafayette

"That was the name," said Lafayette.

"He was my mother's brother," Mr. Porter explained.

"Ah, indeed; well, they were good soldiers and very kind to me when I was wounded. Farewell, young gentleman, I wish you well for their sakes," concluded General Lafayette.

Swelling with undoubted pride from his meeting with the national hero, who had mentioned his father and a relative fighting at his side at one of the iconic battles of the Revolutionary War, J.M. Porter then took a trip to Hanover, New Hampshire.

There he met with the then-president of Dartmouth College, the Rev. Bennett Tylers, stopping at the American Literary, Scientific, and Military Academy in Norwich, Vermont.

Porter's vision of Lafayette College was heavily inspired by his trip to Norwich University, a military academy in New Hampshire which was five years old at the time of his visit. He described it as "a military and scientific institution" and as "a literary and scientific institute." This was high praise to the large, diverse courses of study available to its potential students.

LAFAYETTE (SOUTH) COLLEGE

In fact, as the idea of Lafayette College became reality, inspired by Porter's ideas, more and more kept being added to his vision of what a college should look like, taking in bits and pieces from all his travels and experiences.

Like Easton Union Academy, Porter wanted Lafayette to be non-sectarian in the same way Easton Union was non-sectarian - yet largely run by Presbyterian seminarians. A seminary was one of ideas to be added to Lafayette College.

In Porter's additional wish to include civil engineering to the curriculum - in conjunction with the military engineering program - he aimed for Lafayette College to be only one of a handful of schools in the country to offer such a course of study.

Porter's vision for Lafayette was that of a liberal arts college, with an engineering wing.

But what may have been the biggest driving force of Porter in the establishment of Lafayette College was a democratic view of higher education, which was not universally shared by everyone at the time. He wanted not just the elites of Easton to participate in the college, but the sons of tradesmen as well.

Pulling again from the worldview of Easton Union Academy - which was founded with the idea of "educating poor Germans" - he thought the study of English should be emphasized, as well as German, to include the potential education of many farmers and tradesmen in the surrounding areas that didn't speak English.

In a legal speech he made years later, Porter stated that "the names University and College are derived from the Roman appellations of such companies of tradesmen, etc. as they established, called 'Universitates' as constituting one whole, out of many individuals, and 'Collegia' from being collected together."

As a connected lawyer, Porter was close friends with many people in Philadelphia, including the Pennsylvania Society, the American Philosophical Society, and the Franklin Institute. He also shared their same values, wishing to open something called a "Mechanical Institute" in Easton, similar to the Franklin Institute of Philadelphia and modeled after working-class places of adult learning sprouting up in many areas in England.

In a speech he delivered to the tradesmen of Easton in 1835, he didn't mention Lafayette College by name but showed how passionate he was with the idea of an education for all, not just an elite class. "The question you are asked to answer fairly, and truly, is, have you availed yourselves of all the means placed within your reach, to increase your own resources, or to sustain in society, and in the government of the country, that station to which your numbers and moral standing entitle you?... What boots it that our forefathers fought and toiled and many of them fatten their native soil with their blood," he said, "if their descendents should not properly prize the blessings handed down by them? And how can we prize those blessings properly if we will not use every means for increasing knowledge -- intellectual light -- among us?"

Despite Porter's soft paternalistic tone, he had a passion for education with the idea of democratizing it, moving away from the traditional, liberal arts focus of schools like Harvard and Yale, and instead focusing on a new, innovative course load and disciplines.

His idea of Lafayette College, with its local flavor of emphasis on the "living" languages of English and German along with his idea of higher education for all, was, in the end, unique, radical at the time, and innovative.

Perhaps most strangely of all, though, is that James Madison Porter indirectly had a hand in the foundation of Lehigh University in 1865, thirty-three years later. The lives of J.M. Porter and Asa Packer, the founder of Lehigh, would be intertwined in the realm of business.

3. ASA PACKER'S VISION

James Madison Porter is best known as the man who was the dominant force in the founding of Lafayette College.

What is somewhat ironic is his indirect role in Asa Packer's life, the man whose success in business would end up being the foundation on which Lehigh University would be built.

In the height of the Lehigh Valley's heyday regarding coal and railroads, both James Madison Porter and Asa Packer were instrumental in developing the area, making themselves rich - and building up Lafayette College and Lehigh University respectively.

Porter and Packer are probably more similar than Lehigh and Lafayette people might like to admit, and yet their differences also laid the foundation of the rivalry between the two schools.

Right after the War of 1812, Porter founded his lucrative law practice in Easton, which would kick-start his eventual political career as a somewhat maverick politician, not beholden to the party bosses.

He also started one of his first business ventures, undoubtedly using his maps from his days in the surveyor general's office to help in his work.

"As early as 1815, Porter organized a company 'for the purpose of purchasing and working a quarry of slate, of superior quality, situate near the banks of the river Delaware in Upper Mount Bethel township,'" a

Delaware Water Gap Natural Resource Association historical report said. "The company was capitalized at $15,000 selling 300 shares of stock at $50 each. The stockholders, besides Porter, were businessmen of Philadelphia and Easton. The first $1,500 raised was to be used for the purpose of opening a quarry, erecting sheds, purchasing tools, quarrying, and dressing the slate."

Porter had a business plan.

"It apparently was Porter's method to either lease or acquire outright any parcels of land that displayed evidences of promise for slate quarrying in Upper Mount Bethel Township," the report continued. "A random survey of deed books at the Northampton County Government Center in Easton reveals the frenetic activity of James Madison Porter in many fields of endeavor. He not only involved himself in slate, but made similar investments in limestone quarrying, the extraction of iron ore, and coal mining. Even though the slate quarries near Slateford eventually fell into other hands, Porter was probably instrumental in making the start at some sites. The earliest quarrying near the Delaware Water Gap occurred in 1805-1806 and any connection Porter might have had with these efforts have not been conclusively proved. There is proof, however, that Porter was involved with quarrying by 1815."

Porter was an incredibly busy man during the mid-19th century, with his thriving law practice, management of natural resource fields, and his continuing role in growing Lafayette College. He was also the president of a short railway line, the Belvidere Delaware Railroad, and he taught civil engineering class at Lafayette *pro bono* as it struggled to get off the ground.

At least a portion of Porter's fortune during this time came from his early forays into mining natural resources in slate, iron ore, and coal. It helped him establish his thriving law practice in Easton, as well as helping to found Lafayette College.

He wouldn't be the only one discovering the potential of the natural resources of the Lehigh Valley.

Anthracite coal, discovered to be a good burning material to heat houses during winter, led a multitude of fortune-seekers to Mauch Chunk, the area which was the end of Edward Marshall's run during the Walking Purchase a hundred years earlier.

The town of Mauch Chunk (which has since been renamed to Jim Thorpe) was a center of innovation in a multitude of ways and made a host of smart, enterprising tradesmen rich.

Coal would end up becoming the driver of the fortunes of three men that would leave a lasting legacy on Lehigh Valley education: James Madison Porter, Ario Pardee, Senior, and Asa Packer.

Born in 1805 in Groton, Connecticut, Asa Packer began his career as an apprentice carpenter at the age of 17 after moving to Susquehanna,

Pennsylvania. Starting out quietly in his trade and living in a log cabin he made himself, he slowly and methodically built up his wealth, moving to Mauch Chunk in his mid-twenties in 1833, six years after Lafayette College was founded.

Putting his master carpentry skills to use, he built his own canal boat in 1833. His canal boat would carry passengers and freight from Mauch Chunk to Philadelphia, and eventually he would either own or partially own a fleet of boats for transportation, not to mention a lucrative contracting business.

In an 1834 letter to a friend, early Lafayette College student Alexander Ramsey talked about the townspeople who surrounded the early campus, calling them the "mobocracy of Easton." They were the people who were working on the Lehigh Canal, which had been recently built for the purpose of delivering anthracite coal south to Easton and to large metropolitan areas like New York and Philadelphia.

Asa Packer

"Sometimes you will meet a huge 'Goliath of Cath' [sic], sort of a monster, bareheaded and bear-footed, mounted of a 'wee' bit of a mule, his face, legs and apology for a shirt as black as the deepest shaft in Mauch Chunk coal mine, towing one of these boats, alternatively whistling and singing."

It is possible that the 'Goliath' he referred to was Asa Packer, who captained one of these boats.

The coal that he shipped down the canals also may very well have come from fields that would be owned or leased by Ario Pardee.

Ario Pardee, born in Columbia County, New York in 1810, would start his working life on his family farm, taking a special interest in civil engineering.

Pardee got into the coal business initially by conducting a land survey to forge the path for the Beaver Mountain Railroad, eventually becoming superintendent of that railroad and, ultimately, a coal operator at Hazleton, the site of the richest vein of anthracite coal in the region.

Interestingly, one of the ways Asa Packer expanded his wealth during this time as well was to buy or lease coal fields in and around Mauch

Chunk. It is strikingly similar to the way James Madison Porter bought and leased slate fields in and around Easton.

Ario Pardee

There is plenty of evidence that, while not exactly friends, Porter, Pardee and Packer were business associates who were very aware of each other's actions.

Perhaps the most striking thing about the three men was that they shared a similar vision of the value of anthracite coal, and they jointly understood the importance of civil engineering to delivering their goods efficiently to major metropolitan areas in New York and Philadelphia.

All three used their skills to develop the Lehigh Valley into its prosperous heyday.

Porter knew where coal could be found in Pennsylvania, from his time as a youth in the land claims office. He had forged a thriving law practice, was extremely well-connected politically, especially in Pennsylvania, and was known throughout the region as a skilled lawyer. If anyone could cut through the legal red tape to make railways a reality and pave the way for the future, it was J.M. Porter - and if history would be any guide, he'd find a way to profit from it, too.

Pardee knew that anthracite coal was a commodity that would only grow in demand. After all, he had seen coal grow from a little-used resource to one that people could not live without, not only as a source of household heat, but for powering locomotives, and industrial processes, like iron and, eventually, steel.

There were times when coal did not seem like a commodity that would make a person prosperous, especially when its delivery was dependent on unreliable canals and Mother Nature. But Pardee stuck with it, knowing that he was right, and eventually, black anthracite coal would be able to make it to other markets more easily, making him rich.

By the 1850s, he, along with Asa Packer, were the two biggest coal operators in that part of Pennsylvania, working "hand in hand" to bring prosperity to the Lehigh Valley, according to popular accounts of the period.

Having once been a canal boat captain himself, it must have been very clear to Asa Packer the limitations of using canals as the primary method of transport of coal from the fields to the major cities. The going was slow, taking days to deliver it all by mule more than a hundred miles. In the winter, the canals and locks would freeze, making the way unpassable.

He knew the future was in railroads to deliver coal and passengers, and he would make a sizeable bet with his own money, which he had built from his days transporting, and, later, owning and leasing coal mines, that he was right. Surrounding himself with trusted, brilliant engineers like Robert Sayre and E.A. Douglass, he knew he could accomplish his goals.

By April, 1846, the Delaware, Lehigh, Schuylkill and Susquehanna Railroad Company was incorporated in the Pennsylvania legislature for the purpose of setting up a railway in the area, despite strong legislative opposition.

One of the initial subscribers of stock in the railway company was none other than James Madison Porter.

By 1851, Asa Packer had become a key stockholder in the company as well, and James Madison Porter was elected president.

Porter would have been the perfect person to run the railroad company in the early stages, when legal battles with the canal-based Lehigh Coal and Navigation Company, along with battles in the state house over incorporation (not to mention other railroads), would have required his expertise.

He also led the company in a critical five year stretch, when Asa Packer was to conduct a land survey to create a road for a railway from Mauch Chunk to Easton, where the coal from Packer's and Pardee's fields could connect to the Central Railroad of New Jersey and to New York City.

Robert Sayre

The road would connect two existing railways, the Belvidere Delaware Railroad and the Beaver Mountain Railroad, which was surveyed by Pardee before he went into the coal business full time. (In 1853, knowing that the value of the railroad was about to explode, Porter would become president of the Belvidere Delaware Railroad.)

It would connect to Easton by way of Bethlehem, a junction which would also allow other railways from points south, like the North Pennsylvania, to connect to their coal resources.

The path of the railway was not picked for the Rivalry between Lafayette and Lehigh, but for the placement of the tracks, running along the

Lehigh River from Easton, the gateway to New Jersey and New York, to South Bethlehem, gateway to Philadelphia and points south.

The railway would bring prosperity and economic growth to South Bethlehem that would allow it to consider the construction of a new University.

But it didn't come easy.

At one point, through legal delays, the railroad charter nearly expired. The road construction, which Packer himself led, suffered through delays and strikes, and a cholera outbreak.

There was labor unrest, where, as the story goes, Asa tried to break a picket line and was thrown into the Lehigh River by the striking workers.

There was also the engineering issue of crossing the Delaware River to connect three different railroads at two different grades and elevations. Packer put his right-hand man, Robert Sayre, on the job, where he designed an engineering marvel, connecting the different railways via a double-decker bridge and a curving, sloping track.

Through the efforts of all these men, eventually the road, and the railway, which would be renamed the Lehigh Valley Railroad, was finished by 1855, connecting the "black diamonds" of coal to the New Jersey and New York markets, and extending the already-substantial fortunes of all three men.

And when the nation descended into Civil War in the 1860s, the demand for coal, iron and steel exploded further.

From its incorporation in 1846 to 1870, Porter, Pardee and Packer would all be on the board of directors of the Lehigh Valley Railroad at different points.

The railway would also fuel the economic growth of both Bethlehem and Easton - and would become a critical means of transportation between the two cities, fuelling the football rivalry long after the time when anthracite coal ruled the Lehigh Valley.

During the time the coal economy was booming in the Lehigh Valley, Lafayette College was struggling.

After setting up Lafayette's charter of incorporation in 1836, and an incredibly challenging laundry-list of disciplines and fields of study, it took six years for Porter to convince the legislature to fund an appropriation for his academy, and six years to narrow down the daunting, lofty goals of education to a plan that could actually be executed.

One of the more intriguing people to decline the early presidency at Lafayette was Friedrich List.

List was a leading economist of the time, and firm believer in the

"American System," a three-pronged economic theory which stated the best chart for growth would involve a strong national bank, a protectionist policy of high tariffs on exports, and federal subsidies for roads, canals and infrastructure.

It was a system firmly backed by Alexander Hamilton and the Whig Party, of which Porter was a loyal voting member in the early days.

At the urging of General Lafayette himself, List moved to nearby Berks County, where he set up a successful German language newspaper in a county where Porter's brother was the county judge.

List's vision of higher education was closer to France's National Polytechnic Institute, a system of learning which fit his "American System" philosophy quite well. The system emphasized industry, political knowledge, and the spread of knowledge across the country not through elites, but through a new industrial class.

This worldview also fit Porter's vision for the young college, but for a variety of reasons - including Easton's distance from the bustling metropolis of Philadelphia - List declined to become Lafayette's first president.

Friedrich List

"List was elected, but could not serve," Condit's *History of Easton* said.

With List declining the invitation to be Lafayette College's first president, it would take nearly half a decade for Porter and the trustees to pull together a faculty, a full-time president, and a curriculum for his college, all the while engaging in his lucrative legal practice and managing his many business interests.

It was difficult to lure people to take the position, due to the lack of appropriations. There were no rules on how to found and maintain a college: Lafayette had to figure it out as they went along, and they managed to invent a way to make it happen.

According to the original terms of the contract, the trustees would only provide physical facilities, with the president and faculty dealing with all the financial aspects of the college. There weren't millions coming from the state, or one large, wealthy benefactor: the president would need to fundraise and would have no financial backstop.

Not many presidents were willing to take on that challenge, but finally the Rev. George Junkin, who had designed the classical curriculum at Columbia and headed the Manual Labor Academy at Germantown, PA, accepted the position.

Rev. George Junkin

However, as a part of his conditions for accepting the presidency, he would fundamentally change Porter's vision.

He replaced military training with a system of manual labor training, which was unsuccessful at Germantown but thought by him to be able to make work at Lafayette. He also replaced a non-sectarian, semi-technical course load with one that was similar to the classical one he taught at Columbia. It was also somewhat sectarian in nature, having the course "Evidences in Christianity" added to the curriculum with the Rev. Junkin teaching the class.

In 1832, Lafayette College would open its doors, very different from the initial, grand visions of its founder, James Madison Porter - but it would be open, with Porter and the Rev. George Junkin running the college.

Mr. Porter's institution, named after a Revolutionary War hero but without formal military training, was finally up and running.

Once in session, though, it was still a challenge for the college to be a success.

From the get-go Lafayette was looking for funds from the state to keep the place running.

Two early ideas of funding of the college did not work: the first, having the students work as laborers to generate income for the university, and the second, getting a subsidy from the state to allow Lafayette to become an agricultural college. (The request for the subsidy was declined by the Commonwealth of Pennsylvania.)

These struggles had a spiral effect on the school. Without adequate funds, the school couldn't fund enough equipment for some of the sciences for the technologies of that era, notably civil engineering, chemistry and geology. And without enough study materials, fewer students enrolled at the school, making the funding problems worse.

Lafayette, now primarily a Presbyterian school to educate young men for the ministry, was in trouble.

The Civil War hurt enrollment at all institutions of higher learning, but Lafayette's enrollment was decimated. As was common among colleges at the time, some Lafayette alumni fought for the Union, and others fought for the Confederacy. (Ario Pardee's son, a civil engineer, fought for the Union Army and became a war hero.)

Only four professors remained at Lafayette during the Civil War, and they worked for free while President William Cassidy Cattell, a passionate Presbyterian minister, looked to outsiders to finance the college in 1864 while the war was raging.

Pardee Hall, Lafayette College

One of Dr. Cattell's appeals went to none other than Ario Pardee, who wrote him a $20,000 check on the spot, "and, essentially, saved the college," Diane Windham Shaw, Lafayette's current archivist, said in a recent lecture series.

It is not too much to say that Pardee's $20,000 check saved Lafayette. Multiple histories of Lafayette College point often to that check, and the subsequent gifts by Pardee over the next decade, as the key to keeping the college running before its enrollment exploded after the war.

His money helped found the "scientific department of the college," as a writer of the *Lafayette Monthly* put it in 1871.

"Compare the present with the past and see what a change here," it continued, "from a small faculty numbering *four* to one numbering *twenty-six*; from an institution embarrassed on every hand, and struggling for long years to maintain an existence, to one comparatively free and established on a firm basis."

At about the same time Pardee was saving Lafayette, Asa Packer was approaching the Episcopalian bishop of Bethlehem, William Bacon Stevens, with his idea of founding a university on the South Side of Bethlehem.

"The idea was not suddenly formed," Lehigh's *Twenty Year Book* stated in regards to Asa Packer's wishes in founding Lehigh University. "The establishment of this University was the result of determination long considered. Denied the polish and culture of a university education, he was forced to acquire it by his own energy. Knowing how potent a factor of success such an education became, he determined that the young men of the region in which he acquired his wealth should possess the means of acquiring such an intellectual foundation."

Now one of the wealthiest men in America, Packer wished to bequeath a half a million dollars, and sixty acres of South Bethlehem land, in order to create his educational vision.

The acreage would be just a short walk from the management offices of the Lehigh Valley Railroad.

That would be convenient for Robert Sayre, Packer's trusted right-hand man, board member of the Lehigh Valley Railroad and South Bethlehem resident, the man who would be charged with the details of executing Packer's wishes for his polytechnic school.

Aside from reasons of convenience for his trusted "detail men," Packer also was motivated to put his university in Bethlehem due to the changing nature of its inhabitants.

"'Bethlehem' and 'Moravian' are almost synonymous and whenever you read a description of one or the other you will find an abundance of such adjectives as "quiet," "peaceful," etc.," Lehigh's *Twenty Year Book* said. "These were eminently characteristic of the people who built the quaint old town on Bethlehem hill, though that town is almost a thing of the past, owing to the destruction of nearly all the houses of the last century and the influx of people of other communions."

Coal, iron, railways, and steel were changing the old Moravian town to one of industry. This had caused a new population to settle there, one looking for industrial jobs that rewarded hard workers.

As Lafayette's ideals in education encompassed James Madison Porter's 1826 vision, Lehigh's ideals reflected Asa Packers' 1865 view of what a school should be.

His vision was one of a "polytechnic university," a school where the students would learn the ways of business and industry, without neglecting the classics - in its way, a different, unique sort of institution of higher learning, similar to other polytechnic universities being formed at the same time - MIT, Stevens Tech, and the Worcester Polytechnic Institute.

Unusual for a technical school, Lehigh was to have a "School of General Literature" to teach the arts, making it more than just a trade school.

Dr. Edward Coppée, Lehigh's first president, explained further.

Coppée wrote Lehigh's first curriculum, writing that the new University was to be "the means for imparting to young men of the Valley, of the State, and of the Country, a complete professional education… The system determined upon proposes to discard only what has been proved to be useless in the former systems, and to introduce those important branches which have been heretofore more or less neglected in what purports to be a liberal education."

You could say that Packer's vision for Lehigh was that of an engineering university, with a liberal arts wing.

Knowing that Pardee donated $20,000 to save Lafayette College and add an Engineering wing to their school around the same timeframe, it begs the question: did the foundation of Lehigh come about in any part due to a rivalry between the two men?

There is a story, recounted by the historian David Bishop Skillman in *The Biography of a College*, that there was a time (presumably around 1864), where Ario Pardee approached Asa Packer with the idea of adding an engineering wing to Lafayette College.

So the story goes, Packer refused Pardee's offer after learning that Lafayette was run by the Presbyterians, who turned their nose up at him when he was a young entrepreneur in Mauch Chunk looking for a church to attend.

It's impossible to prove whether the meeting actually happened, which would have occurred at a time when Presbyterian Lafayette was only able to survive through the largesse of Ario Pardee. The fact that Asa Packer donated the princely sum of $500,000 for the foundation of an Episcopal University a few stops down on the Lehigh Valley Railroad certainly might strike some as a spiteful move.

It was also the largest donation for an institution of higher learning at the time, something worth remembering. (Put in perspective, it would be the equivalent of more than $7.5 million 2012 dollars.)

However, the timing of this story is suspect.

Packer had made his intentions known to Sayre well before Pardee's fateful meeting with the president of Lafayette. Every recounting of Packer's founding vision for the university states that it was his intention for a long while to create a new university, not forge an engineering wing to an existing college.

Furthermore, there are no other signs in the history of Asa Packer, Ario Pardee, or the family of James Madison Porter, that these men had any sort of personal rivalry between them in terms of business.

In fact, there is plenty of evidence - not least from the history of the Lehigh Valley Railroad - that they had to work closely together to develop their complex web of businesses in the Lehigh Valley.

Asa Packer's and Ario Pardee's coal and business interests frequently intertwined, and Pardee was a major stockholder in the Lehigh Valley Railroad. Both men became rich with the success of the railway.

And you could also say that Packer's greatest industrial achievement, the establishment of the Lehigh Valley Railroad, could not have come to pass without Porter's early leadership and vision to get the company established.

THE LEHIGH UNIVERSITY.

We can only prove that Asa Packer, a devout Episcopalian, frequently worked with, and collaborated with, people like Ario Pardee and James Madison Porter who were themselves devout Presbyterians.

It is true that early on in their histories, Lafayette and Lehigh were aligned with different sects of Protestantism – Lafayette Presbyterian, Lehigh Episcopalian.

But the rumor of the religious views dividing Asa Packer and Ario Pardee, whether true or not, was used to fuel the rivalry between the two schools, and from the day Lehigh opened its doors, they were competing with Lafayette for students.

The words "discarding what was useless" from Coppée certainly seemed like a direct rebuke of the history of Lafayette, which had tried many different models of operation to survive. One would have to assume that the people running Lafayette did not see their evolution as "useless."

It also wouldn't be a surprise that a rumor started from Easton about Asa Packer, especially after hearing that he was donating half a million dollars to start a university. It couldn't have made people at Lafayette very happy, considering they were going cap in hand in order to survive.

Lafayette also considered themselves somewhat of an engineering school, despite their liberal arts curriculum. Well before it was popular, James Madison Porter taught some civil engineering courses at Lafayette, arguably the first of their kind.

One can imagine that Lafayette didn't just see Lehigh's polytechnic school as a competitor, but as a threat to their survival as a school.

That competition became clear when Lehigh University would open its doors to students for the very first time.

The original plan was to open Lehigh in 1867 or 1868, when Packer Hall would be completed and ready to accept boarding students.

But sometime in 1866, the trustees of Lehigh decided to open that September.

"A probable reason for the change was that Packer wanted the advantage of opening first, before students could go to Cornell or Lafayette, both of which were served by the Lehigh Valley Railroad," Willard Ross Yates noted in *Lehigh University: A History of Education in Engineering, Business, and the Human Condition*. "Ezra Cornell and Andrew White were fast organizing their school at Ithaca; and Lafayette was on the verge of beginning [comprehensive] instruction in engineering and applied science with Pardee's money."

Packer Hall

The founding day of Lehigh University was hurried in order to better compete for undergraduate students that may have gone to Lafayette College. The Rivalry was on.

4. ATHLETICS COMPETITIONS BEGIN

The first football game between Lehigh and Lafayette came about in 1884, only twenty years after Lafayette nearly closed its doors, and only eighteen years after Lehigh's first incoming class of thirty-nine students.

During that time, some of the first intercollegiate athletic contests were being held between the two schools.

It was a world emerging from a terrible, bloody Civil War. Sports of all kinds were entertaining and distracting the country. Athletics mania swept through the nation, and the excitement engulfed the campuses of Lafayette and Lehigh, too.

From these seeds, a sporting Rivalry between Lafayette and Lehigh sprouted rapidly and intensely in an area that had been the source of political rivalry and education rivalry.

In the 1870s, all walks of life were caught up in the craze of amateur sports, and the college-going students in the Lehigh Valley were no exception.

One reason for this surge of popularity in athletics came from across the Atlantic in the form of literature.

Published in 1857, the novel *Tom Brown's School Days* described the adventures of a young boy at an English boarding school, including a description of schoolyard sports games. (One vivid account involved an early version of a sport that would be the foundation of modern rugby.)

The author, Thomas Hughes, toured the U.S. in the 1870s in support of his wildly popular account, talking specifically about education and intercollegiate sports.

Illustrations from Tom Brown's School Days (French edition, 1875)

The book was hugely popular in America, and was also very influential concerning American views of education, and the place of physical activity as a part of that education.

(The book also, eventually, helped spur the idea of developing codified rules for sports such as rugby and soccer in England, which didn't have set rules from a national association prior to the 1860s. Eventually, this zeal to lay down rules for sporting events carried across the ocean to America as well, cumulating in the development of a set of standard rules for an American version of "foot-ball," as it was then called.)

The oldest colleges and universities embraced the idea of intercollegiate athletics first, with Harvard, Yale, and Princeton organizing some of the first amateur modern sports and intercollegiate teams.

When word of their boat regattas, athletic associations, gymnasiums and sporting events spread from local and national newspapers, the students at both Lehigh and Lafayette wanted to follow suit.

Early versions of *The Lafayette* student newspaper not only referred to the latest athletic developments at those schools but also mentioned *Tom Brown's School Days* on occasion, noting its popularity. The student writers seemed heavily influenced by the book, wishing to model their school's existence around an ideal boarding school type of experience - which, of course, involved sports.

"When foot racing, base-ball playing, and rowing are moderate," one student author said, "and have for their object the permanent improvement of the physical man, in order that the mind may have a healthy dwelling-place, they are to be encouraged; but when the body must be trained without any regard to the mind, and for the sole purpose of coming off victorious in a severe physical contest, it is time for intelligent people to pause, and use every endeavor to cause all such exhibitions to appear in their true character."

"There is much valuable time consumed by many college students during the whole of their college course," the article continued, "in learning to handle the oar skillfully and gracefully. In order to belong to the best crew in a college much devoted to boating, a student in most cases not only must spend a large share of his time actually rowing, but he must use other means for giving his muscles the necessary power and tension, and his body the proper weight. He must be a frequent and regular visitor at the gymnasium, and there carry out the ideas of training which he has already spent much valuable time in acquiring. He must prepare his body solely for a rowing match, and not for what his Creator intended it - a beautiful dwelling for an immortal soul."

Such sentiments aside, both Lehigh and Lafayette students had especially noticed Harvard's recent intercollegiate competitions with Yale involving rowing sports, reading about them in newspapers. As a result, the student bodies at both schools were eager to develop their own navies and have regattas of their own, and pressured their faculties accordingly.

On both campuses, the desire to compete in athletics intercollegiately was seen as inextricably tied to the establishment of a gymnasium.

Harvard built a state-of-the-art gymnasium in 1859, in part to develop the physical attributes of their student bodies, but also to identify potentially strong oarsmen so they could beat Yale at their annual regatta.

Lehigh's *Twenty Year Book* says the students, even from the very first student publications, clamored for the trustees to arrange the building of a gymnasium.

When the trustees dragged their feet on getting one built, students took matters in their own hands.

"The subject was not allowed to rest with petitions but, in the bedrooms of some of the undergraduates who lived in Packer Hall, there grew small gymnasia where the muscular element was developed," the *Twenty Year Book* says. "In 1874 the south-east room in the fourth floor of Packer Hall was given by the President to a club selected from the various classes and by them fitted with rings, horizontal and parallel bars, clubs, dumb-bells and other appliances and in this room there was a steady and uniform system of exercise during the greater part of the year."

"Unfortunately for the club," the account continued, "the building was not made for such a purpose and, after loosening the plastering in the lecture-room of the Professor of Engineering, below, the club and its apparatus was without a local habitation, the name alone remaining."

Starting in 1868 and continuing yearly throughout the 1870s, Lehigh students petitioned annually for a gymnasium to be built on campus.

Similarly, Lafayette students, too, petitioned for a gymnasium in spite of faculty opposition.

As early as 1872 a student writer on *The Lafayette* wrote on that subject, "That a gymnasium has been wanted we do not deny," but throughout the 1870s their battle to get one built was equally as fruitless as Lehigh's.

"With our increasing numbers and prosperity," a Lafayette student writer noted, "its necessity was never so forcibly impressed upon us before. The students must have exercise, and in the absence of a gymnasium to resort to for physical training, they will have recourse to means which are not altogether creditable to our college as a Christian institution. We do think an earnest effort should be made to have a fine gymnasium on College Hill."

Rutgers vs. Princeton, 1869, Hale Center Mural

Despite their lack of gymnasiums, both Lehigh and Lafayette document evidence of students taking part in largely spontaneous athletic contests on their campuses during this time.

In the early days, the graduating classes were the main organizational unit of the students. Freshmen bonded with their fellow freshmen, and sophomores their fellow sophomores, and the classes would compete against one another in different sports. In the early days, inter-class competitions were more passionate competitions than intercollegiate ones.

The intramural competitions would take place in baseball, racing, and a relatively new sport, a modified version of English "foot-ball." The rules were still fluid, still somewhat loosely based on the soccer-themed "foot-ball" type game played for the first time on the campuses of nearby Princeton and Rutgers.

There are official records of early versions of football being played on the campuses of Lehigh and Lafayette in the 1870s, against different graduating classes in a mostly unstandardized way.

"The football of my day [1873] resembled the soccer of today," one early Lafayette trustee told Francis A. March, Jr. in the history *Athletics at Lafayette College*, with another also confirming that one of the pickup games played between the classes was the early form of "foot-ball."

His description corresponds with the type of "foot-ball" contested in 1869 between Rutgers and Princeton in what is considered the first-ever "foot-ball" game played between two institutions of higher learning.

There was also a huge amount of local interest in a brand-new American sport that was sweeping the nation at that time - baseball.

On Lafayette's campus, baseball quickly developed into a sport that the student body embraced enthusiastically, starting off by competing intramurally, and, eventually evolving into a college-wide team that would compete against local semi-professional teams such as the "Easton Professionals" and a "professional team from Brooklyn, NY called 'The Nameless,'" according to *Athletics at Lafayette College*. (No word if the name of "The Nameless" was actually a team called the "Dodgers.")

But it would be games against Princeton and Lehigh which would become the ones that would unite the members of the Lafayette student body - and give Lafayette students somewhere to go with their dates.

Thanks to the Lehigh Valley Railroad running multiple trains daily to and from Bethlehem and Easton, Lafayette and Lehigh students could run into each other often in the 1870s.

The combination of a ½ hour train ride - and a steady supply of eligible female college-age girls at nearby Moravian College - would make Bethlehem a popular stop for the all-male students of Lafayette, whose student body was three times the size of the university in South Bethlehem.

The historic Sun Inn, a former Moravian meeting house, was a popular place for both Lafayette and Lehigh students for meetings and dances.

The first description of an intercollegiate sporting event with some sense of Rivalry with Lehigh came in the October 1875 edition of *The Lafayette* school newspaper, where one of the students described a meeting on the diamond between teams representing both schools.

"It was the first game that our new nine has played, and taking all things into consideration, they did remarkably well. We would, however, preferred to see the score 16 to 1, instead of 16 to 4."

Later in the same edition, they mention in great detail a return baseball game with Lehigh in Bethlehem, which helps explain how, even in 1875, the Rivalry between the two schools became so intense.

Sometime in 1875, 150 Lafayette students accompanied the baseball team on the Lehigh Valley Railroad to Bethlehem, "anticipating a glorious victory," *The Lafayette* mentioned.

But Lehigh had allegedly enlisted the pitcher and the catcher of the local semi-pro baseball team, the Bethlehem Crescents, to suit up for their side, making it a much different contest.

"The first uniform for the University nine," Lehigh's *Twenty Year Book* notes, "was adopted in 1875, after the colors brown and white were chosen. It consisted of a white suit and cap with brown trimmings, and a brown-edged shield with the year and L.U. upon the front of the shirt."

Lehigh's choice of school colors might have been influenced by Lafayette's decision to choose maroon and white as their school colors, which they had done on January of that same year. "Lafayette participated in the first 'American Intercollegiate Oratorical Contest' in New York City, sponsored by Mrs. John Jacob Astor and other prominent New Yorkers," Lafayette's website explains. "This is the first known intercollegiate contest for which Lafayette needed to display school colors. It is said that President Cattell himself chose Maroon and White for the event."

With the Lehigh University bell brought to the grounds by the home teams' students to celebrate the anticipated victory, the team in the new brown and white uniforms saw their plans for victory take a turn.

"In the eighth, Lehigh made two runs," *The Lafayette* continued. "Affairs now assumed an ominous look, and our easy victory of two to one 'wasn't there.'"

Down by a run in the top of the ninth inning, Lafayette's prospects looked grim, but there was a glimmer of hope, according to the student newspaper.

"Two men by good hits, aided by bad plays of the Lehigh's, made second and third. The excitement is now intense," *The Lafayette* continued breathlessly. "Coffin is at the bat; one, two strikes; a shiver runs through the crowd, Lafayette is gone; but hark, click goes the bat, a neat daisy-cutter is sent with a vim from his sturdy arm out between second and first where no one can stop it, and the two men on bases run it."

The game tied, catcher W.G. Coffin supplied even more drama.

"Cheer upon cheer rent [sic] the air, and 'La-fay-ette" was heard loud above all in the din," the account continued. "Coffin, happy name for *us*, but indeed a *coffin* to the hopes and aspirations of Lehigh University Nine, stole round to third base, and on a low passed ball went home, and thus won the game."

Once Lafayette retired Lehigh in the bottom of the ninth, the celebration was spontaneous.

"The Lafayette boys carried the player on their shoulders up through the town of Bethlehem," it continued, "singing Lafayette songs as they went. As they came in front of the Moravian Female Seminary, they let off a goodly portion of the pent-up feelings in lustly cheering for the fair inmates who had assembled in large numbers at the windows to watch the strange sight."

The account is the first vivid description of a sporting contest between both schools that went beyond the reporting of the score, or merely a snide remark about the other school. It demonstrates that the games between

Lafayette College Baseball Team, 1875

the college and university carried more weight than ordinary sporting contests - fueled by proximity, their regional differences, and the important presence of girls.

As for Lehigh, though they tried very hard to be Lafayette's equal in baseball, in their *Twenty Year Book* they talk tersely about the baseball aspect of the Rivalry from their viewpoint.

"[In base-ball], our only rival of any prominence at that time was Lafayette College, and we are sorry to say that our efforts have been uniformly unsuccessful in that direction," it said.

While the dreams of Lafayette and Lehigh students' athletic programs had at their roots the ideas of regattas and rowing competitions, ironically, both schools did not end up with successful navies.

Neither school ever competed in any races, as maintaining boats were prohibitively expensive, and the Delaware and Lehigh rivers were not ideal for competitive crew.

Both Lehigh and Lafayette showed interest in track and field events, however, and had plenty of level, straight running tracks on which to practice - the towpath canals alongside the Delaware and Lehigh rivers.

Track and field events were an outgrowth of the popularity of Greek physical culture that the students were attempting to emulate. The popular educational philosophy of that time was that a whole education, ostensibly like that of the ancient Greeks, involved education of the mind, body, and spirit.

Like baseball and rowing, track and field was another sport that was starting to capture the fascination of many institutions of higher learning.

The Eastern Intercollegiate Athletic Meet at Mott Haven, New York was becoming a very popular spectator sport. Harvard, Yale, Princeton and other major Eastern colleges were in attendance, and new events were being added all the time, such as bicycle races and tug-of-war competitions, that gave more ways for a college to be crowned intercollegiate champions.

As the 1870s progressed, some educators were slowly starting to feel that the education of the body was being neglected in favor of pure scholarly pursuit. Amateur track and field games in particular were seen, therefore, as an extension of the education of the body, largely undertaken through the organic efforts of the students themselves.

Not all faculty members took this view. Others felt that sports were too distracting from the main purpose of being at a college or university, which was to learn.

The debate between faculty members on the subject was largely scholarly in nature, though, since the sports were still being run and conducted by the students themselves.

There is plenty of evidence that organized track and field meets emerged from impromptu athletic contests held between students on both Lafayette's and Lehigh's campuses. One former Lafayette student described "stunts" of track and field records and events in the book *Athletics at Lafayette College* which predate Lafayette's formal track and field records.

While Lehigh couldn't manage to defeat their nearby neighbor in baseball, they found in track and field where they could equal them - and eventually beat them.

In 1876, the newly-founded, student-run Lehigh Athletic Association, or L.U.A.A., was formed with the idea of supporting the students' athletic activities.

Organized by a student, Edward. H. Williams, the L.U.A.A. was funded by having students voluntarily donate $10 to subscribe and participate in athletics. (It was Williams who organized the first athletics meeting to determine Lehigh's school colors, and it was Williams who designed Lehigh's first baseball uniform.)

By the end of the 1870s, the L.U.A.A. was also sponsoring track and field events at Rittersville Driving Park, a racetrack for horses about four miles west of Bethlehem towards Allentown.

The students would take a horse-driven bus from South Bethlehem to Rittersville, where there was an oval for biking and horse races, and the team would find out who were the best athletes.

"Those taking part in the contests met at the Eagle Hotel in Bethlehem and were driven in an omnibus to the park," one early track and field athlete recollected in a *Lehigh Alumni Bulletin* of 1920. "Those taking part in the events knew nothing of training, had no trainer or coach, ate anything they fancied and lots of it. Imagine eating a heavy meal and going four miles from the University to Rittersville Park to take part in an athletic meet, but we did it."

These track and field events in nearby Rittersville did not go unnoticed by the residents of Easton and the students of Lafayette.

"In the matter of athletics, Lafayette College is extremely weak," an April 1880 *Easton Express* editorial said. "She is always conspicuous for her absence from the reports from Mott Haven. Why is this? There is a magnificent campus for practice in athletic sports. We trust a new life may be infused into the athletics of old Lafayette."

This time following Lehigh's lead, Lafayette would found their own athletic association only one month after the editorial was written, electing a student president, adopting a constitution, and setting dues at $2 per student. (With a large student body, there was no need for dues to be more expensive.)

Ultimately this interest would spur an intercollegiate track and field meet between Lehigh and Lafayette. The very first took place in 1881, where Lehigh won twelve events, Lafayette won ten events, and there was one tie.

"We have to record a defeat in our contest with Lehigh University," the *Lafayette Journal* lamented back home after the meet. "A defeat, too, doubly humiliating, coming as it did, from an adversary in every other respect our inferior... The audience was anything but sympathetic."

In the spring when they had their next meet with Lehigh, Lafayette's defeat was even worse.

"During the last year we have been remarkably successful in athletics," Lehigh's *Epitome* yearbook crooned, "The games between the athletic associations of Lehigh and Lafayette, held last May in response to a challenge from the latter college, mark an era in the intercourse between these institutions."

In their write-up of that inter-collegiate track meet, it detailed that Lehigh had won ten events and only lost three to Lafayette.

Two weeks later, Lehigh athletes would then make the trip to the Eastern Intercollegiate Athletic Meet at Mott Haven, New York, where they'd have national success that accompanied the large defeat of Lafayette.

Interior of Coppée Hall Gymnasium, Lehigh

"Four men competed in the pole vaulting," *The New York Times* reported. "Soren, the Harvard man, led off with 8 feet; O. Harriman, the Princeton boy, with 3 inches better; F.W. Dalrymple, of Lehigh, went an inch still better, and the bar was kept going up peg by peg until Dalrymple won by vaulting 8 feet 9 inches."

The Brown and White had "carted off two gold and one silver medal [sic], giving us the third place among our sister colleges in athletics; Columbia and Harvard only outranking us." the *Epitome* said.

The three medals, a gold in pole vaulting, a gold in the 120 yard hurdles, and a silver in shot put, were sources of great pride for Lehigh's students.

(Bronze medals were not issued in those days.)

And just as baseball success had allowed Lafayette to develop a strong sense of school pride, track and field success had allowed Lehigh to feel like they were able to be the equals athletically of their "sister colleges," Harvard and Columbia.

Athletics also allowed them bragging rights over their neighbors to the east, who could not count themselves in that same club in track and field.

It also moved Lehigh's board of trustees into action. They finally green-lighted the construction of a gymnasium after years of inaction.

Artist's Rendition of Lafayette Gymnasium, 1884

Thanks to student pressure, the support of President Robert A. Lamberton, and the success of the Lehigh athletes at Mott Haven, Lehigh would finally have a gymnasium that would allow them to compete with Harvard and Yale not only in track and field, but many other sports.

By the end of 1883, Lafayette's president, Dr. William Cattell, in his final act as president, announced that a fund had been raised for the building of a new gymnasium.

The building committee decided to use the plans from the gymnasium built at Vanderbilt University for their on-campus building, with the only change being that it would be five feet wider.

In *The Biography of a College*, a full early history of Lafayette, it stated, "This was the fulfillment of a student wish that had been expressed more loudly, more insistently in each successful year of his great administration."

What *Biography of a College* didn't say is that the final push to get Lafayette's gymnasium built was from Lehigh's brand-new gymnasium, freshly finished in March of that year, built on their wins against Lafayette and the other prominent Eastern colleges of the time at Mott Haven.

5. THE VERY FIRST FOOTBALL GAME

In the beginning, the Rivalry existed in several sports. When they faced off, whether it was in track or baseball, when one beat the other it was a special cause for celebration.

But once football was instituted at both schools, the true Rivalry really started to kick into high gear.

The football Rivalry has spawned bonfires, parades, torn-down goalposts, bits of sod ripped from the turf, and grandstands burned, or torn up.

Perhaps the football Rivalry stems from the physical nature of football, the placement on the calendar, or the proximity of both schools. Even from its earliest days, it was heart and soul in its intensity.

Lehigh hated to lose to Lafayette in baseball. Lafayette was humiliated when they lost to Lehigh in track and field events. But all those things seemed to dwarf in comparison to the football Rivalry, which kicked off in earnest in 1884.

The same year Lehigh and Lafayette started their football Rivalry, the cornerstone for the Statue of Liberty was laid down on Beldoe's Island.

In 1884, the first streetlights powered by electricity illuminated Easton. "Electric lights now burn brightly in Easton's streets," *The Lafayette* noted in November, 1884, "and in many of her business houses and places of amusement." (South Bethlehem wouldn't get them until 1887.)

In 1884, Mark Twain lived in a house just outside Hartford, Connecticut, a Victorian Gothic mansion where he and his family settled after he had penned *The Innocents Abroad.* That year, in the upstairs billiards room, he wrote *Huckleberry Finn.*

1884 was the heart of what was considered "The Gilded Age," based on the book co-written by Twain and Charles Dudley Warner. It represented an era of congressional gridlock, lack of strong presidential leadership, and big business filling the void in the form of railway companies. (The Lehigh Valley Railroad was one such big business, as was Pardee & Co., Ario Pardee's coal interests.)

VIEW OF "THE POINT" AND UP THE DELAWARE, 1886.

The president at that time was an ailing Chester Arthur, who was ending his term as the 21st president of the United States as he was suffering from Bright's disease, a kidney ailment. He elected not to run for another term. In November, Democrat Grover Cleveland defeated Republican James Blaine in a presidential campaign that was filled with mud-slinging.

It also would be year of the first-ever meeting between Lehigh and Lafayette on the gridiron, only a couple of years after the early collegiate athletic powers of Harvard, Yale, Princeton, and others had established standardized rules for "rugby football," as it was still called at the time.

"Foot-ball" was not unknown to either campus before their fateful first few meetings.

"With the class of 1884 came football in the modern sense to Lafayette," Francis A. March, Jr. wrote in his history *Athletics at Lafayette College.* "Every afternoon during the fall, the whole college turned out for a sort of soccer game. It was seniors and sophomores versus juniors and freshmen. It was good fun and good exercise."

"In the fall of 1881 football occupied the student attention as never before," David Bishop Skillman wrote of Lafayette in his *Biography of a College*. "One great difficulty was to learn the 'Rugby' rules. The first attempt to play a game under these rules was on November 15th, 1881, when the class teams '84 and '85 met on the campus."

Francis A. March, Jr.

The person who Francis March credited for bringing football to Lafayette College was Theodore L. Welles, who would go on to become a successful engineer in the Lackawanna Iron and Coal Company.

"I had played with the Wilkes-Barre Academy and the Princeton Freshmen of the class of '83 before coming to Lafayette, and as I was very enthusiastic for the game, proceeded to get it started for the class of '84," he recalled to Francis March. "During my time in college, we had no regular trainer or training table, and all the training received was an endeavor by [teammate H.L.] Craven and myself to make the players keep good hours, refrain from beer and other intoxicants, get out to practice and run after practice from two to three miles a day around the circular track on campus."

The first game Lafayette would play against an outside entity would be Wilkes-Barre Academy, who would face off against the freshman class of 1885. "The game was played in a driving rain which froze as it fell," *Biography of a College* noted. "The game lasted from 2:30 until after dark and was lost, as it was averred, because neither the freshmen nor the officials knew the rules."

Their campus being about fifty miles from where the first-ever game between Princeton and Rutgers was contested, Lafayette students eagerly read the news of the athletics exploits of schools like Princeton, Rutgers, Penn, Columbia, Harvard, and Yale in Lafayette's school paper.

With the class of 1884, Lafayette students clearly wanted to build up their own athletic program to compete with those schools, undoubtedly encouraged by reports of big intercollegiate games. "The gate receipts for Yale's [1881] Thanksgiving game exceeded $1,400," Skillman's *Biography of a College* noted in regards to football's popularity then.

Lafayette's very first intercollegiate games in 1882 were against Penn and Rutgers, ending with the Maroon and White not scoring a single goal in either contest. *The Lafayette* does not offer a description of either game, though Welles recalled those two games and two others against Stevens Tech and Haverford, which were both victories.

"I recollect with what curiosity the youngsters of the town looked upon that oblong leather-covered article," faculty member and staunch Lafayette foot-ball fan Francis March recalled in his *Athletics at Lafayette College* of that first home game versus Penn, "and discussed pro or con whether it was better than the old association ball used up until that time."

The setbacks against the best teams in the nation at that time did not dampen the spirit of Lafayette students, instead inspiring *The Lafayette* writers in 1883 to implore their foot-ball team to train better.

"The foot-ball team have made great improvement for the practice they have had," one student editorial reported, "and have made faithful efforts to practice. This is what is needed. Not less practice that the colleges that have given enthusiastic attention to foot-ball for years, but twice as much. There is no reason in the world why we shall not have an effective a team as any, when the men get used to it and can work together like veterans, and play the game that their strength and fearlessness would indicate."

Lafayette's hard work would pay off with their first two official victories recognized in Lafayette's archives.

Quarterback Jacob D. Updegrove guided the Maroon and White to victories against Rutgers and against an early incarnation of a team from Bucknell, while a future general that would serve during the Great War, Francis' brother, Peyton C. March, would suit up as fullback.

"The game of November 10th, 1883 with Rutgers was one of the most laughable ones that I have ever experienced," Theodore Welles recalled to March in *Athletics at Lafayette College*. "There was three to four inches of slushy snow on the field, and we were very averse to playing the game. They insisted, however, so upon my orders the Lafayette team appeared on the field in all the old suits they could muster, carefully refraining from wearing the jersey suits which we had secured for the season. The ball speedily became water-logged and it was impossible to kick it, but we succeeded in making four touchdowns to Rutgers' none. After the game, the reason for their determination to play came out in the statement that, as they had been beaten every game that year, they thought they could come up and beat Lafayette anyway."

Buoyed by their first-ever victory, a Thanksgiving trip to Lewisburg resulted in a thorough beating with the Maroon and White's first-ever victory against Bucknell, 59-0. With Welles not even playing, the Maroon and White cruised, up 44-0 at halftime during which "the ground was in a miserable condition," notes *The Lafayette*, "the mud making running and dodging extremely difficult."

Jacob D. Updegrove

("The *Lewisburg Mirror*, on the football-game with Lafayette: 'We might call it a triumph of intellect over GENIUS.' - as it were," *The Lafayette* also noted.)

Perhaps it was these first two Lafayette wins, or perhaps it was simply because J.S. "Jake" Robeson played the game at nearby Germantown Academy, that Lehigh took up the sport with the idea of starting an intercollegiate team mere weeks after Lafayette made a spectacle of Bucknell.

While not technically the father of football at Lehigh, Richard Harding Davis, a renowned journalist, author and world traveler, was a member and tireless spokesman for Lehigh's first football teams. He didn't only participate in Lehigh first intercollegiate team - he also played in the first class-based games in 1883 that would predate Lehigh's intercollegiate one.

Davis, a strong athlete, won the "hurdle race" his sophomore year in the fall meet by five seconds, as well as the high jump at 5 feet and ¾ inches.

Later known nationally for writing in *Harper's Weekly* about the exploits of the Rough Riders in the Spanish-American War, as well as the German march on Brussels, Davis is known as the template of the "foreign correspondent," even garnering a mention posthumously in the famous Alfred Hitchcock movie of the same name.

He also wrote extensively about football, and thoroughly loved the game based on his collegiate experiences playing at Lehigh.

When it came to taking credit for starting Lehigh's football team, though, Davis stopped short.

"J.S. Robeson is the father of football at Lehigh," Davis recalled for the *Lehigh Quarterly* of 1891. "It was he who induced the sophomores of the University of Pennsylvania to send their eleven up to play an eleven from the class from '86 on December 8th, 1883, and it was he who captained the Varsity team the following year."

Davis even downplayed his role on the team.

"I was so much more of a spectator than a player in the first games of foot-ball

Richard Harding Davis

at Lehigh that I felt I could not be fairly accused of writing in self-laudation if I accepted the invitation of the editor of *The Quarterly* and told something about them," he said. "My position as spectator was not back of the ropes, but behind the rush line to the right of the quarter, where I had an uninterrupted view of the field and absolute leisure, as the captain, though he did not know much, had at least sufficient judgment to always pass the ball to the other half, and I never got it by any chance unless he fumbled it and someone else did not fall on it first."

Further evidence in *The Lehigh Burr*, the student newspaper, though, shows that Davis was not a bad runner at all, getting singled out for making "quite a number of excellent runs" in the interclass games of that time.

In the December 8th game of 1883 between Penn's sophomores and Lehigh's sophomores, won by Penn, 16-0, one of the referees was a student from Lafayette, who undoubtedly must have informed Lafayette's athletic association that Lehigh had a "foot-ball" team.

It would be the following year, 1884, when Theodore Welles, now captain of the Maroon and White, would first approach Robeson to challenge the vastly inexperienced Brown and White to a game - the first meeting between the two schools.

Welles was shrewd in asking Lehigh for a game - he knew that it would be difficult to replicate last year's Maroon and White football successes with many of their key players graduating, though their star quarterback, J.D. Updegrove, was still leading the team. A team like Lehigh would be exactly the tune-up their team would need before competing against the national powers of Penn, Princeton, and Stevens Tech.

Despite the presence of Robeson and the Davis brothers on Lehigh's squad, the rest of the squad was very inexperienced.

FOOTBALL
OPENING GAME!
LEHIGH UNIVERSITY
vs.
LAFAYETTE!
COLLEGE CAMPUS,
SATURDAY, OCT. 25, 1884
AT 3 O'CLOCK P. M.
TICKETS   •   •   25 CENTS.
Daily and Weekly Free Press Steam Job Printing Office, 12-16 South Bank Street, Easton, Pa.

"As simple as the game was then, the Lehigh men knew even less of it than any other team in the country," Davis reflected for the *Lehigh Quarterly*. "When the Varsity took the field in 1884, Robeson, Knorr, Bradford, and [his brother Charles] B. Davis were the only men who had played the game before, and in the first match with Lafayette, which was the first University game played by Lehigh, the other seven men had learnt what little they knew of it in three weeks' practice on the class elevens."

Undaunted, Davis used his charms to convince Lehigh to pay $52 for eleven striped brown and white jerseys, complete with brown and white stocking caps. The team elected J.S. Robeson captain, chiefly, according to Davis, due to him owning the only foot-ball jacket in the school. It was his jacket which was the pattern for the other jerseys he had made at a local shop.

"With this idea we went down to Easton," Davis recalled in the *Lehigh Quarterly*, "where we thought what we did not know about the game was not worth learning."

Back then, according to *The Lehigh - Lafayette Legacy* by Todd Davidson and Bob Donchez, fields were 120 yards long, and not necessarily cleared of debris. Admission to the game was collected from a field officer along the sidelines, though many spectators got around paying the admission because the playing area was not enclosed.

Strangely, there are no detailed accounts from either student newspaper of the very first game between the two schools, though *The New York Times* described the first game in that year: "The first inning was very interesting, as Lehigh frequently got the ball dangerously near Lafayette's goal line, but each time was beaten back, the point being made by the home team."

Davis' remembrance of the game was colorful.

"The score of that first game was 52 to 0, and my chief recollections of it consist of personal encounters with the spectators and Easton policemen, who had an instinctive prejudice to Lehigh men which they expressed by kicking them on the head whenever one of them went under the ropes for the ball," Davis said in the *Lehigh Quarterly*. "We knew so little of the game that only one man had strips [primitive cleats] on his shoes and the rest of us slid over the worn grass as though we were on roller skates."

In fact, inexperienced Lehigh was the only team Lafayette managed to defeat in the 1884 season. After beating the Brown and White with ease, they would be dominated by the incredible score of 140-0 at Princeton four days later.

Lafayette would have another opportunity to play Lehigh that season, and gain another victory.

The next game was played in Bethlehem, on a Wednesday at Lehigh's athletic grounds, and would be the site of Lehigh's first-ever intercollegiate home contest.

The athletic grounds, located off of Brodhead Avenue, was on more of an open field than Lafayette's intimate campus setting, but also had a turf that was filled with "rocks and broken bottles," according to Davis.

That game also ended in a Lehigh loss, but to the student reporters of

The Lafayette it still didn't feel like a great victory.

"The brilliant prospects with which the season opened have been clouded by one defeat after another... the Lehigh team seems to be the only one we can defeat," they reported.

In contrast, Richard Harding Davis was very encouraged by the fact that the Brown and White had actually scored in the second game, which Lehigh lost 34 to 4.

Who scored that first-ever touchdown for Lehigh? None other than Richard Harding Davis.

"He often declared that he took keener satisfaction in making that first touchdown for Lehigh than in all the short stories and verses he ever wrote," a friend recalled in letters many years later.

There were also the antics of the Lehigh fans - who decided to declare victory in another way.

"We did not win... but we did give Lafayette the worst lickin' she ever had and many, many a sore head went back to Easton that night," a proud Lehigh alumnus recalled for the *Lehigh Alumni Magazine* many years later.

As for Lafayette, they were not satisfied with simply sweeping Lehigh.

"Two years ago we played our first game of foot-ball," *The Lafayette* reflected. "Since then we have been active in this game. Last year we put out a strong team, but unfortunately for us, seven vacancies were caused by graduation. This year's eleven is largely composed of men who never played the game until this season, and, although we have lost nearly all the games thus far, yet with one exception we have had the satisfaction of good scores."

6. THE RIVALRY INTENSIFIES

When you look at the student accounts of the early games of football at Lafayette and Lehigh, you can see instantly the ones involving their nearby neighbors are a bit different than the others.

"October 18th. Lafayette played a game with Dickinson College of Carlisle, PA," a typical non-Lehigh game account in *The Lafayette* starts. "The game was called at 12:30 and only thirty-five minute innings were played. One of the most noticeable features was the absence of kicking and bad blood."

"The foot-ball team opened the season on Saturday, Sept. 29th with a game at Princeton," an 1888 non-Lafayette account from *The Lehigh Burr* recounts. "A number of Lehigh men accompanied the eleven and returned greatly pleased with the work of the team and the prospects for a successful season."

By reading the write-ups of these early games between Lehigh and Lafayette, and comparing it to the tame, respectful accounts of games against other schools, it's easy to see the hotly contested nature of the Rivalry games – games that, seemingly, almost always ended in controversy.

In 1885, Lehigh and Lafayette's football programs were each trying to achieve different goals.

Lafayette, with a two year head start on Lehigh, was trying to prove that they belonged in the Intercollegiate Football Association alongside the national powers of the time, Harvard, Princeton, Penn, Columbia, and Yale.

On the other hand Lehigh was simply trying to get their program off the ground, first by securing a win against their neighbors from Easton, then working their way towards a winning season.

In this era, there was no regulation as to whom schools could schedule. Football schedules ranged anywhere from six to fourteen games. Schools could play other intercollegiate teams, or instead face off against "athletic clubs" consisting of local sports fanatics.

Schools could also schedule teams multiple times during the season, which was of great benefit to both Lafayette and Lehigh since they were separated by a quick train ride and could easily arrange trips for their fans to attend the games.

Accounts of the games, too, sold a lot of papers in the Bethlehem and Easton areas, especially with the early bitterness and controversy of the Rivalry.

In the early going, that bitterness and controversy led to incomplete games, with one side or the other walking off the field.

The first of what was to become many of these types of games took place in Bethlehem on October 31st, 1885.

"During the first inning Lafayette had to face a very strong wind and the sun, which was shining brightly," *The Lafayette* says. "Previous to the game, the captains of the respective teams and Mr. Posey, the referee, had a conference. In it the Lehigh captain expressly desired the referee to allow as little roughness as possible."

As the game was played, Lehigh's star center, W.R. Pierce, was "disqualified for deliberately butting into Lafayette's halfback, [E.E]. Davidson," according to *The Lafayette*. "Lehigh refused to stand by the referee (their own selection) for enforcing the very thing they had requested."

After Lehigh's captain, Harry W. Frauenthal, protested the call to no avail, "with five minutes left in the first half, Lehigh refused to continue play and left the field with the score 0-0," the book *Legends of Lehigh - Lafayette* says.

"Later, football authorities awarded the game to Lafayette by a 6-0 score, stating that Lehigh had no right to protest the game on a referee's judgment call," *Legends of Lehigh - Lafayette* continued.

It wouldn't be the first time calls were questioned, or independent third parties consulted, in matters of football games between the two schools.

The return game on November 21st, too, the first-ever tie in the series, also had a questionable call at its core.

With the Maroon and White up 6-0, "by this time, it had become so dark that the referee was unable to see well enough to render fair decisions.

It was owing to this that Lehigh was enabled to tie the score," *The Lafayette* reported.

"Davidson had carried the ball within 25 yards of Lehigh's goal when he was tackled," they explain. "He called down, and the referee had acknowledged that he had heard him do so. As Davidson was putting the ball down, preparatory to snapping it back, Howard of Lehigh grabbed it, ran down the field, touched it down and claimed a touchdown which the referee allowed, contrary to all rules."

Such results are not a surprise considering there were still many questions as to the rules of the game from both the players and the students officiating the games. There wasn't a centralized authority for setting rules, and any questions would take weeks to answer, if they even knew who to ask.

These two controversial endings were only the tip of the iceberg.

In 1886, Lafayette was on the brink of establishing itself in the top tier of football schools of its era. The Maroon and White would be on their way to a 5-0 start, establishing their first-ever win over the best intercollegiate team in the state, Penn, 12-0, and their second-ever win over Rutgers, 24-2.

The games versus Lehigh, though, were the contests that were the talk of the town.

The first game against Lehigh, played in Bethlehem, ended with the score 12-0 in favor of Lafayette. It was called midway through the second half due to a torrential downpour that caused the "players to be rolling about the field," *The Bethlehem Times* reported.

"The game was witnessed by a large audience, Lehigh being especially well represented," *The Lafayette* stated. "The game was very close and exciting in the first half, but in the second half Lehigh was going to pieces rather rapidly when time was called. Lehigh, having given up all hope of scoring as it was raining very hard at the time, asked that time be called. Lafayette wanted to go on with the game."

Even though it seemed like the score of that first game was settled, it wasn't.

"Now after thinking about the matter for a day," *The Lafayette* continued, "[the referee] wants to change his decision and declare the game a tie. If he did not know enough to decide correctly and stick to his decision when he had given it, why did he try to referee?"

Making matters worse was that the referee was a Lehigh student, who nonetheless wrote the preeminent expert on all things football at that time, the former Yale football player and pioneer of the game, Walter Camp, for a clarification.

"The rules require two halves of 45 minutes each," Camp wrote to him, "so technically a game is no game unless full time is played. 'Rain or shine' is the custom among footballists, so the leaders might have insisted upon continuance of the game or forfeit. As they did neither, the referee must call it no game."

Despite the esteemed Walter Camp ruling in favor of Lehigh, the Brown and White, perhaps sensing how unseemly the whole situation was, thought the game should be awarded to Lafayette because "Lehigh was clearly outplayed by its opponent," *Legends of Lehigh - Lafayette* said. "In the archives, the game is officially recorded as a 12-0 Lafayette victory."

The controversy of the rainy November 6th contest would pale in comparison to that of the game of November 24th, however.

The meeting in Easton occurred on Lafayette's new-looking athletics grounds, which saw enthusiastic students take matters into their own hands by cutting down the trees surrounding the athletic field prior to the big game against their nearby rival. "Although the trees were a great nuisance to the football ground," *The Lafayette* chastised, "we disapprove of the method by which the students got rid of them. This summary way of proceeding partakes too much of the savor of lawlessness."

Walter Camp

Lehigh fans probably thought the lawlessness applied to the officiating during the game in Easton.

"From the opening whistle, it was apparent that Lehigh would not get any breaks," *Legends of Lehigh - Lafayette* mentioned. "H.L. Forceman, the manager of the Lafayette team, acted as referee. The Lafayette players were suspected by the Bethlehemites of playing unfairly during the game, breaking many rules and deliberately trying to injure the Lehigh men."

According to *Legends of Lehigh - Lafayette*, Lafayette was routinely given four or five downs to Lehigh's three.

"At one point, Williams of Lafayette intentionally kicked captain Pierce of Lehigh in the back when he was down," *Legends of Lehigh – Lafayette* said. "No penalty was called by the Lafayette referee and play continued."

The straw that broke the camels' back involved the only score of the game.

"During the second half, a dispute occurred over what down it was for

Lafayette," *Legends of Lehigh - Lafayette* continued. "The referee went to the sidelines to consult with a substitute and an *Easton Daily Times* reporter. According to one source, while the referee's back was turned, a Lafayette man picked up the ball and ran the ball to Lehigh's three yard line. After the commotion, the referee turned to the action on the field. Upon seeing the result, he cheered with undisguised enthusiasm for his team, allowing the play to stand."

Pierce, undoubtedly outraged at the course of events, protested, but the play stood.

As the Lehigh players were on the sidelines putting on their sweaters, leaving the athletics grounds, a Lafayette player picked up the ball and touched the ball down in the end zone.

From Lafayette's perspective, it was unconscionable that Lehigh would protest, considering Lehigh's only non-loss against the Maroon and White came on a similar play in 1885. In that game Lafayette accepted their fate and swallowed their 6-6 tie.

"The same old chestnut," *The Lafayette* reported. "Lehigh was badly broken up, and left the field rather than suffer an invariable defeat."

But Lehigh felt that the referees had it in for them in Easton, and found it outrageous that Lafayette was awarded a touchdown after their team had left the field of play. To the Brown and White, for all practical purposes, the game was over, or at least stopped.

"We regret that Lehigh and Lafayette are unable to play a game of football on Lehigh's grounds without getting into a dispute and breaking up the game before it is finished," a student reporter at *The Lafayette* wrote. "It is a most lamentable state of affairs when two colleges like Lehigh and Lafayette, situated so near each other and whose relations ought to be of the most intimate kind, cannot play a friendly game of football without so much ill feeling on both sides."

(It was an ill feeling that lingered. Lafayette scored it a 4-0 victory, while Lehigh's official records called it a 0-0 tie. It would be more than a century later when Lehigh would finally change their official records to score it a 4-0 win for Lafayette.)

Lafayette would end the 1886 season with a 10-2 record, their only defeats coming from powerful Penn in Philadelphia, 20-10, and then-potent Wesleyan, 26-0.

The wins over Lehigh notwithstanding, Lafayette's goal to be mentioned in the same breath as Penn and Princeton had been attained, and it would be the first step on their national rise to prominence.

The idea of the Championship of Pennsylvania hadn't been conceived yet, but if it had, Lafayette's 1886 team could have won it.

As dominating as Lafayette was over Lehigh in those early games, in the late 1880s the tides turned dramatically due to a play devised by the founder of Lehigh's football program.

Perhaps unsurprisingly, the origins of the play have also been disputed with a distinct Rivalry flavor.

The "V Trick," or "Lehigh V," as it's known in South Bethlehem, was a revolutionary play in college football at the time.

It involved eleven men forming a "V" with interlocked arms to direct the mass of the entire team against a hapless weak link on the opposition's line, and the halfback running behind the rush line.

This was especially effective after a kick, since the ten men would be able to run forward and get a head of steam going, applying their mass momentum to make larger gains.

To some, it was the basis of all the mass momentum plays that followed, such as the infamous "Flying Wedge" implemented by Harvard in the 1890s.

Though it would ultimately be banned, mass momentum plays like the "V Trick" were an important historic milestone in the evolution of college football.

The origins of the play come down to who you believe: Richard Harding Davis, the former Lehigh football player, or Parke H. Davis, the former Princeton and Lafayette football coach.

Parke Davis, in his historical book *Football, the Intercollegiate Game*, credited the "V Trick" to a former Princeton player who attended the

University a few years prior to when Davis was a lineman there.

"Strange to say," P.H. Davis said, "this highly ingenious and complicated formation was not the result of long and laborious study, but was conceived suddenly in the crisis of a close game and put into immediate execution. This game was the contest between Pennsylvania and Princeton, October 25th, 1884, and the inventor of the play was R.M. Hodge, '86, of Princeton."

Hodge's claim in P.H. Davis' book was during the course of this game, "if the rush-line would jump into the shape of a V with the apex forward and with Baker [the halfback] inside, the formation ought to gain ground." The formation was then allegedly tried once, then shelved for the Yale game, and then shelved for several years afterwards.

Richard Harding Davis pointedly disagreed.

"I want to recall the fact that it was at Lehigh when the V Trick was first attempted," he recalled for the *Lehigh Quarterly.* "It was invented by Jake Robeson, and first tried against Pennsylvania with the success which now always accompanies it."

The Pennsylvanian, Penn's student newspaper, describes the contest where it was allegedly first unveiled by Lehigh on November 18th, 1886.

"On Thursday, what was supposed to be our foot-ball team was beaten at Bethlehem by Lehigh, by 28 to 0," the writer said. "The Lehigh rush line is strong, and heavy. Each member of it singles out an opponent, and sticks to him the entire game, no matter where the ball is. When Lehigh has the ball, each man on her line wraps his arms deliberately around his opponent, while a Lehigh half-back runs with the ball. As Lehigh was much heavier than we are, she had little difficulty in winning."

Walter Camp, the legendary college football authority of the time, credited Lehigh with coming up with "the first practical working of it" in *Spalding's Official Football Guide of 1891*, a point that Richard Harding Davis mentioned prominently in the *Lehigh Quarterly.* "Walter Camp, the Yale coach, always credits Lehigh with this trick when he writes," he said.

What wasn't in doubt was the "Lehigh V" took the Brown and White from tackling dummies for Lafayette's football team to being a very strong football team in their own right.

In 1887, despite an 80-0 walloping by Princeton in the first week, Lehigh shut out both Swarthmore and Dickinson in subsequent games, setting up their first match in Bethlehem with high hopes that they could bust through, finally, against Lafayette.

"The Haverford men had a bad impression of Lafayette before they came," *The Lafayette* noted, "and that such an impression was given them by some of the students at Lehigh 'University.' Such talk would naturally emit from the 'University' men, whose brains are soaked with athletic jealousy. The Lehigh 'University' students know well enough that they have always, when on the Lafayette campus, been treated with courtesy and they know just as well, that the same treatment has not always been extended to Lafayette."

The Lafayette, too, seemed to think that Lafayette had their best chance yet to be beaten by the 'Lehighs', as they were sometimes called. "Next Saturday, unless something unforeseen happens, we play Lehigh," the student reporter said. "The result of the game is in considerable doubt. A large number of men should accompany the team to South Bethlehem and give them the necessary encouragement."

Lafayette was right to be concerned, as Lehigh got their first-ever win in the series by a score of 10 to 4.

As ever, though, the win was not without controversy.

"For the first time in foot-ball history Lehigh defeated our team," *The Lafayette* lamented. "About two hundred students and several members of the faculty accompanied them. [Lehigh's] Corbin made a touchdown and the umpire smiled approval. Play was rather sharp for the next few minutes neither side having the advantage, until finally Corbin, assisted by the referee, made another touchdown."

Of particular interest to the newspapers of the time was an alleged discussion between the referees calling the game, with a Lafayette fan saying that they overheard one say to the other "we will do Lafayette dirt this half."

"In the second half Lafayette played a good game, but in every point the referee favored Lehigh," the student writer at *The Lafayette* continued, "while the umpire was a useless figurehead. During this half of the game Van Loon secured the ball near Lehigh's line and would have made a touchdown. The referee at first gave the ball to Lafayette, but afterward changed his decision and gave it to Lehigh. Williams made a touchdown that was not allowed. W. Van Loon secured a free catch directly in front of Lehigh's goal and Payne kicked a beautiful goal from the field; not allowed. The game soon afterward closed."

The Lehigh Burr had a different view.

"The manner in which Lafayette, after having been defeated in a perfectly fair game of foot-ball, attempted to put all the defeat on the referee, cannot be too highly condemned by the college world," the writer said. "If they had taken the defeat in good grace, nothing would have been said, but when they set to work to deliberately besmirch the reputation of the referee, we feel compelled to speak in his defense. Mr. Spalding, as was Mr. Miers, was perfectly fair, and we can, without hesitation, declare that all his decisions and rulings were perfectly impartial and fair. How, after the abuse that has been showered upon Mr. Spalding, Lafayette can expect to obtain an unprejudiced referee, we cannot see."

"The Lafayette man who was willing to make an affidavit [in the Easton paper] that he heard the referee say to the umpire, 'We will do Lafayette dirt this half,' has not as yet been found, nor is he likely to be," *The Lehigh Burr* account continued. "But there was one thing amid the mass of abuse contained in the *Easton Express* that speaks well for Lehigh, and that was: 'Considering the bitter feeling which exists between the institutions, the Lafayette men were treated well.' That a Lafayette man under any circumstances would admit such a thing, would be a high compliment, but when one admits it, when they were defeated, is the highest praise ever given to Lehigh by any one. Lafayette men should take the matter into their own hands and see that those who report athletic contests with other colleges, for the Easton papers, should not wander hopelessly away from the paths of verity."

The Lehigh Football Team of 1887

Walter Camp decided in 1887 to implement the rule that two paid officials for every college football game, one referee and one umpire, be mandatory. The officials at the earliest games between Lehigh and Lafayette, who frequently were students of the home team, and the electric criticism in the local newspapers, may have been a few of his reasons. (It wouldn't stop the criticism of biased officiating in the Rivalry, but it would mandate some basic rules of impartiality, for example, having the officials come from a neutral third college, such as Princeton.)

Lafayette got the better of the Lehighs in the return match in Easton, a 6-0 game that was "severely contested, yet never had we seen one in which greater good feeling prevailed between the contestants and also between the friends of the opposing elevens than in this," said *The Lafayette*. "One of the pleasing features of the game was the absence of slugging," *The Lehigh Burr* also reported.

At the end of the 1887 season, both student papers took time out to contemplate the history of the early Rivalry.

"The interest that Lehigh men take in the Lafayette-Lehigh foot-ball games is remarkable," *The Lehigh Burr* noted. "Ever since the first game has been played a large number of men have accompanied the team to Easton. So large a number go that special rates are always granted on the railroad, and twice, a special train. This is an excellent thing; it encourages the team, which knows that it is not playing before a hostile or at the least an unappreciative audience, and tries to do its best. When the team goes farther than Easton, of course the number of men who accompany it is fewer, but at the same time there are always quite a number that go, and [we] hope that this will continue to be the case."

With Lehigh and Lafayette knowing that the games between the two were special, both were already thinking of ways to demonstrate that fact for the 1887 season.

Both student papers declared their teams the unofficial "Champions of Pennsylvania" under different criteria.

The Lehigh Burr claimed that Lehigh's 4-3-0 team split the mythical championship since they split their two games against Lafayette.

The Lafayette, on the other hand, said that the 7-2-0 Maroon and White were the true champions, since they split against Lehigh but beat Penn (and Lehigh lost to Penn).

There was no way to determine such a champion that season.

The idea of a competition for the Championship of Pennsylvania would carry through the next few seasons, but the warm feelings and the "absence of slugging" between Lafayette and Lehigh would not.

It also didn't prevent a future version of *The Lafayette* publishing this bit of prose about the "V" formation, either.

> Break, break, break.
> That awful revolving V!
> For every yard that they make that way,
> They make by walking on me.
>
> Oh! Well for the man who's at full-back!
> He never gets into the play;
> Oh! Well for the extra half!
> Who is stationed five yards away.

But the LAFAYETTE men go on.
Till our line resembles a wreck;
But oh! For a whack at the man with the ball,
And a chance to jump on his neck!

7. THE CHAMPIONSHIP OF PENNSYLVANIA

Until 1888, Lafayette had dominated Lehigh for the most part in football.

Lafayette was still way behind the best Princeton teams of the era, but they were consistently competitive with Penn, and had mostly gotten the better of the Brown and White.

In 1888, the tides would turn dramatically in favor of Lehigh.

Though the Brown and White would lose decisively to the two national powers on their schedule, Penn and Princeton, each subsequent week Lehigh, behind the rushing of Amherst transfer Samuel Warriner and increased effectiveness of the "Lehigh V," would get stronger.

Before their trip to Easton, they posted back-to-back shutouts against Penn State, 32-0, and then-powerful Stevens Tech, 10-0.

Clearly looking to be the first team to ever beat Lafayette twice in the same season, *The Lehigh Burr*, was taking no chances.

"On the eve of our game with Lafayette," they said, *"The Lehigh Burr* would like to make a few suggestions to the students and the team. First - let every student accompany the team to Easton and give them encouragement in every way possible. Second - systematic cheering led by four seniors appointed for the purpose. Third - under no circumstances encroach upon the field, for you will be as liable to interfere with your own team as that of Lafayette, and once started it will be impossible to keep men of both colleges off the grounds. To the team, we wish you success. Be sure that a reliable referee and umpire are on hand before you leave Bethlehem. Give the umpire no cause for declaring a foul when near your opponent's goal!"

Undefeated Lafayette had every reason to be confident as well.

"Our foot-ball team has not been beaten this year," *The Lafayette* said. "We hope this will not make them overconfident. Last year we lost the game to Lehigh on account of overconfidence. It makes a team neglect to practice. In playing a game our team only plays hard when absolutely necessary to keep the other side from scoring."

The Brown and White would come out of the gate with a quick score.

"The Lehigh audience had scarcely realized the merits of this fine run, before [fullback Samuel] Warriner was seen making for the goal line in his usual good style," *The Lehigh Burr* excitedly reported, "with only one man to stop him. The result, as may be imagined, was a touch-down squarely behind the goal posts. Dougherty kicked the goal, and confusion reigned supreme on the Lehigh side of the field. Time, 25 minutes. Score, 6 to 0."

This would wake Lafayette up, however, as soon thereafter the Maroon and White's halfback, E.B. Camp, would score to make it 6-4 before halftime.

In the second half, yet another officiating controversy would occur - and another fight.

Samuel Warriner

"After another gain, four downs gave Lafayette the ball," *The Lehigh Burr* reported, "and Camp started it the other way by five yard increments. What might be termed 'a lively scrap' took place about this time among the rival players, and the spectators showed a decided tendency to take a hand also, but the excitement was finally quieted, and the field cleared again for action."

Tense throughout, it was inevitable that the officials would be in the middle of the outcome.

"Twice Lehigh's backs were forced over the line while the crowd went wild," *The Lafayette* reported, "thinking the referee could give nothing else than a safety, but [Lehigh's QB] Corbin said he heard "down" before the line was crossed and Lafayette gave in. Lafayette kept up their hopes during the last three minutes, so near did our team have the ball to Lehigh's line, and only gave up when, with 40 seconds left Camp tried for goal from the field and failed —final score, Lehigh 6, Lafayette 4."

There is one photograph of that game that survives, which exists as a part of the Richard Harding Davis archives. It shows men in stocking caps, standing, facing off against each other at Lafayette's slightly sloped quad.

"Lafayette's contingent could scarcely believe their senses," *The Lehigh Burr* said, "but Lehigh grasped the situation and the players in one and the same instant. The victorious team was carried from the field amid the liveliest manifestations of joy from the Lehigh delegation, and the cheer for the Brown and White rang through the streets of Easton as it never had occasion to ring before."

After the loss and another the following week, Lafayette's hopes for a mythical Championship of Pennsylvania and another win over Lehigh would be dashed.

Injury decimated the Maroon and White after the Lehigh game, which may have led to their thrashing by Penn, 50-0. Travelling to Bethlehem, spirits were low, and Lehigh finally was able to sweep their bitter rivals, shutting out Lafayette 16-0.

The exploits of Warriner and Corbin were not the big takeaway from the game, however.

"After the 16-0 victory," the book *Legends of Lehigh - Lafayette* said, "the Lehigh freshmen celebrated by setting fire to the grandstand. The torching of the grandstand was not only a victory celebration, but a way of demolishing the old grandstand so that a new one could be constructed. The Lehigh students had long viewed the old grandstand as an eyesore and a disgrace to their Athletics Grounds."

The local fire departments were alerted to the fire, which was a three-alarm blaze, though when they realized it was the grandstands, they let it burn out. The lone exception, according to *The Bethlehem Times*, was Easton's fire department, who had the attitude, "It's only Lehigh, let it burn!"

Even with the sweep over Lafayette, Lehigh's status as the "Champions of Pennsylvania" was not unanimous. In a matrix appearing in *The Lehigh Burr*, it showed that Lehigh (2-1) and Penn (2-1) tied, with Lafayette (1-3), the only one out of the race.

The official "Champions of Pennsylvania" title would have to wait until 1889, when both athletic departments would turn away from track and field as a way to compete against each other. Their primary fall athletic focus became America's fastest-growing fall sports passion, college football.

"A silver cup has been offered by Mr. R.P. Linderman, Lehigh '84, as a trophy of the foot-ball Championship of Pennsylvania," *The Lehigh Burr* reported in that year. "Designs for the cup have not yet been prepared but it will be very handsome, of massive silver, while special care will be taken to secure a design

Paul Dashiell

thoroughly artistic and appropriate, and the cup will be fully equal to any college trophy of the kind ever offered. The [articles and conditions drawn up for the Championship] is not intended to form a foot-ball league, such a thing being deemed unnecessary, but to provide such general regulations as will fairly determine the state championship."

Amidst the aftermath of the Johnstown flood, which killed thousands of Pennsylvanians in May of that same year, a college football series between the three Pennsylvania schools took on greater meaning, with the outpouring of sympathy about the disaster from all across the United States.

The Championship of Pennsylvania was founded in part to kindle the interest in football at both Lehigh and Lafayette, but it also may have been a way to lock in Penn to playing return games in the Lehigh Valley, as they had already cancelled these games against both Lehigh and Lafayette in the past.

With the additional excitement involving a championship to play for, both Lehigh and Lafayette started the 1889 season in rough fashion.

The Brown and White would lose three of their first four games, including two to Princeton - but by much less lopsided scores in the past, 16-0 and 16-4. It would be the first time Lehigh scored against the Tigers in their history. ("The [Princeton] students all thought that the score of the Saturday before was discouraging enough, but the climax was reached when it was learned that the Lehigh team had scored against the 'Nassau Boys,'" *The New York Times* said about the second game.)

Despite those defeats, the loss in the first game of the Championship of Pennsylvania series would sting the most, falling to Penn 6-4 after the Brown and White's brand-new 22 year old halfback from Johns Hopkins, Paul Dashiell, couldn't play due to a thigh bruise.

"The game at Philadelphia with the University of Pennsylvania was as poor an exhibition of foot-ball as we have participated in for a long time," *The Lehigh Burr* admonished. "Loose playing abounded on both sides and there was hardly a pretense of teamwork. While our team was badly crippled by the absence of several of the best players, the wretched blocking and tackling of the old men was everywhere noticeable, and such as would not be tolerated in a practice game."

But there was more to Lehigh's loss than met the eye.

"In the first game for the Championship of Pennsylvania, there were on the opposing team three graduates, two of whom were married men, and none of whom were on the rolls of the college represented or in any way connected with it," a later issue of *The Lehigh Burr* reported. "There is no remedy for this injustice but in the concerted action of the colleges immediately concerned, yet as the general sentiment is markedly in disfavor of such practices, it is to be hoped they will not long continue. The tendency toward professionalism, so marked of late years is one of the gravest evils, and if unchecked will not only bring college athletics into general ill-repute but will destroy their truly excellent purpose just as it is becoming fairly recognized."

The student criticisms of Penn's team might have been a bit more convincing had Dashiell been a student at the time he was at Lehigh. By the time he came to Bethlehem, he had already received his Bachelor of Arts from Johns Hopkins in 1887, and was acting in the role of teacher, well on his way to studying for a Ph. D. in chemistry. According to Francis A. March, Jr., Lafayette students considered him, essentially, Lehigh's first paid football coach. "They were more afraid of Paul Dashiell than they were of the rest of Lehigh put together," he wrote in *Athletics at Lafayette College*.

(Though there were no rules at the time against teachers or coaches playing on the school football teams, students and press members were starting to take notice, even though with the better football teams it was becoming common practice. Across the country the requirement that the players be amateurs, and undergraduate students, started to gain ground.)

Lafayette had problems of a different kind during the 1889 season.

Facing off against Columbia, who had just restarted football after a five-year hiatus, the Maroon and White had a disappointing 10-10 tie at the Berkley Oval grounds, made worse by the fact that "when the men turned in after the game, they found that their pockets had been rifled and money stolen from nearly every man," *The Lafayette* included in their recap.

Playing on the road extensively, another of Lafayette's pre-Lehigh games was scheduled against Princeton. On the day of the game, however, the official declared the field unfit for play, and called the game a "no contest" before the Tigers paid Lafayette's guarantee for making the trip. Before leaving, though, some prankster cabled Easton, where students with baited breath were waiting for any scrap of information about the game. The prankster said the score was 0 to 0 – implying the game had started. Though *The Lafayette* noted the prank, it was not stated whether the perpetrator was ever caught.

As the first game between Lafayette and Lehigh in Bethlehem approached, Warriner and Dashiell were developing into a powerful 1-2 punch.

The first meeting of the two schools in 1889 shows a flavor as to how the games were played in the early days of football.

It was a thrilling game, with Lafayette jumping to a relatively large 10-0 lead when Lehigh came roaring back behind Warriner and Dashiell, the Brown and White scoring a touchdown and kick conversion to make the score 10-6 at halftime.

Crowd control, and keeping any sort of order, was an enormous challenge.

"Everybody, who knows anything about foot-ball," *The Lafayette* reported, in response to criticism from the Bethlehem papers, "or has even seen a game, recognizes the impossibility of keeping a crowd from rushing on the field when a man is hurt or from crowding a little over the line, when an exciting run is being made on the other side of the field. But as for stopping the play of the Varsity men that accusation would seem absurd to anybody who witnessed the game. All the crowding on the field that was done, was done in an orderly way and impelled entirely by curiosity when a man was hurt or some consultation of referees and captains took place. Of course, when touchdowns were made the crowd immediately swarmed out to congratulate their men, but moved back of the lines when play was resumed."

In the second half, Lehigh rode their momentum to score the final ten points in the game.

"The ball remained in Lehigh's possession going steadily toward Lafayette's goal line," *The Lehigh Burr* reported, "until a fine run by Warriner of fifteen yards scored a touch-down for Lehigh in fifteen minutes from the time when play began. Score, 10 to 10. Dashiell punted out to Walker, and he put it down at the ten yard line. Hutchinson and Dashiell each gained two yards. Warriner then scored another touch-down. Dashiell kicked the goal making the score 16 to 10 for Lehigh. The remainder of the half both teams worked hard, and neither had any decided advantage."

While both student papers noted that it was a hard-fought struggle for both sides, *The Lafayette* didn't take the loss well, nor the criticism from the Bethlehem press.

"Lafayette has been abused considerably by the various newspapers since the game with the University for alleged brutal behavior on the football field," they said. "The team itself has not been assailed, but the spectators were represented as a ruffianly mob of toughs who hurled themselves upon the Varsity men at every opportunity, and struck, kicked and generally misused them. The crowd, however, was as far from fulfilling this description as any ever seen at a foot-ball contest. In the front ranks were our professors and the ablest lawyers and doctors in Easton. All the prominent young men were there enjoying the game. Besides these the ground was lined with ladies from Easton, Bethlehem, and other nearby towns, who, if the game had been anything like the accounts, would have been taken from the grounds by their escorts. None of these spectators had the least idea that the game was anything more than an unusually hard-fought contest, and the accounts in the papers were a complete surprise to all."

The Lafayette's account did break down, however, and admit that there was some fighting after all.

"And now, one word about the 'slugging,'" they said. "Everybody knows who began that, Mr. Dewey himself owns up to starting it. We have been wondering why he so openly pursued [Yankee] Sullivan tactics [a turn-of-the-century boxer]. There is but one answer and that forces itself upon us very strongly, that is, he knew perfectly well that Dr. Shell, the referee, would never disqualify a University player. We think the referee was to be blamed for the introduction of any discord that may have sprung from the game. Had there been a man there who could have been relied upon to call a foul whenever a foul was made, neither side would have played foul at all and no disputes would have arisen. As it was 'Doc' Shell was blind to the fouls of the Varsity players and only seemed too loose for those of the Lafayette men."

As a result of the fighting, at future games against Lehigh in Easton, it was vowed that there would be ropes to keep the crowds from spilling over into the field.

"It was said that a posse of police were on hand but were laughed at by the crowd," *The Lafayette* said. "This is humorous. Not a policeman was on the ground, none having ever been required. However, the whole police force will be on hand at our games hereafter, and our friends who come to play with us will have the minions of the law right there to stop any real or imaginary 'brutality.'"

Back in Bethlehem, buoyed by the win over Lafayette and thus rekindling their hopes for the state championship, the Brown and White soared in their next two games against Columbia (51-6) and Penn State by the amazing score of 106-0.

The Nittany Lions, who played Lafayette only two days prior in a 26-0 loss, was seriously undermanned.

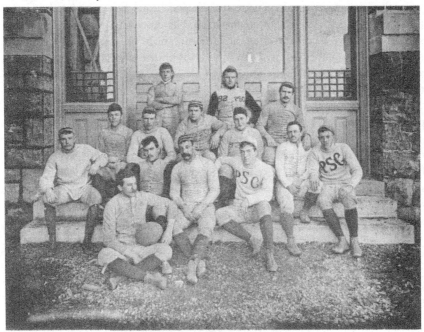

Penn State's 1889 Football Team

"After the game against Lafayette and prior to the game against Lehigh," the Nittany Lion blog *Black Shoe Diaries* reported, "Penn State captain

Charles Hildebrand and two other players went to Philadelphia to attend the funeral of Hildebrand's younger sister. The three men did not make it back to the game until the first half was nearly complete, and Penn State was forced to start the game with just nine players."

The Brown and White wasted no time racking up the score, and took full advantage of undermanned Penn State.

"Play began on the twenty-five yard line," *The Lehigh Burr* said, "and in two minutes Warriner made a touchdown, to which Dashiell added a goal. Four times in rapid succession the ball was carried behind the line, Dashiell scoring the last after a seventy-five yard run through the opposing team. Soon after Warriner on a double pass from Dashiell crossed eight white lines, making the sixth touch down, and the score stood 34 to 0."

While taking full advantage of trick plays like double reverses and also overwhelming them physically, Warriner and Dashielll combined for a remarkable fourteen touchdowns. It was a dominating performance that is unlikely to ever be equaled by another Lehigh football team.

("When the Penn State players returned to campus after the game," the *Black Shoe Diaries* stated, "guard Charlie Aull said, 'We couldn't get at the son-of-a-bitch with the ball.'")

Meanwhile, Lafayette, fresh off their own thrilling win over Penn 10-8, was ready to defend their home turf for the Championship of Pennsylvania.

"The old halls of Lafayette never received more enthusiastic cheers than those which greeted the close of the game against the University of Pennsylvania, and its beautiful campus has never been the scene of a more inspiring sight than the one presented when time was called and the joyous crowd, surging across the field, seized the victorious players and bore them off in triumph on their shoulders," *The Lafayette* reported. "Hats were tossed in the air, cheer followed cheer, ladies waved their handkerchiefs, men seemed to have gone mad. For victory was ours—hard fought, well earned victory. The first game on the campus was won and that a game for the silver cup championship. A large audience of Lafayette, Lehigh and University of Pennsylvania, students and citizens of Easton witnessed the game and both teams received cheering enough to incite them to their most brilliant work."

That's not, however, how the victory was seen by everybody.

"The chief slugging offender, Wells, was ejected from the contest," *Legends of Lehigh - Lafayette* noted. "As a Penn rusher made a dash for the end zone, Wells jumped off the bench and tripped him short of the goal line. After regaining his feet, the Penn rusher charged towards Wells, only to be intercepted by a mob of Lafayette students who left him, according to one onlooker with 'a pair of pretty black eyes, a battered nose, and torn ligaments in his leg.'"

Students bearing "stones and clubs," according to *Legends of Lehigh -*

Lafayette, "chased the Penn team from campus" - which would have serious ramifications later for the Maroon and White.

With Lehigh's place in the Championship of Pennsylvania also in the balance, and Easton's campus a short train ride away, attendance at the game in Easton was overflowing.

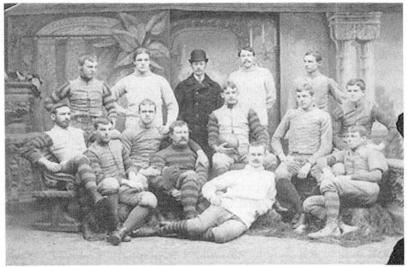

Penn's 1889 Football Team

Lehigh, Lafayette, and Penn were tied 1-1-0 in the State Championship series. Two games remained, including a game between the visiting Brown and the home Maroon in Easton.

The Lehigh Burr, anticipating another hard-fought game, and remembering the issues with the game in Bethlehem, and at Penn, exhorted the Brown and White fans to act in an orderly fashion in Easton, while finding it irresistible to dig at their Rivals.

"The recent disgraceful conduct of the students at Lafayette renders it necessary to say a word regarding the game to be played there to-morrow," they said. "A very large crowd will accompany the team, and the imprudent conduct of a few men may cause serious trouble. Every assurance has been given that the Lafayette students will not assault our players, and in any difficulty that may arise between the teams remember our men are abundantly able to take care of themselves. You are there as spectators only and have no right on the field during the progress of the game. We regret to have to make such an emphatic announcement, but Lafayette's course in the past does not justify confidence in their intentions of fair play, and we earnestly hope trouble will be avoided."

The Lafayette reported that the largest crowd in campus history came to town to watch the game against Lehigh.

"The windows of the halls were crowded with fair faces," they said, "and the roadway was lined with carriages from which a large number viewed the fray. The field had been enclosed by ropes and a number of officers were present so that not the least disturbance marred the pleasures of the day."

Lehigh would get the ball facing the goal on the Maroon and White grounds which had a slight downgrade. This was a big advantage for a half because the afternoon sun shone in the eyes of the defenders, a well-known feature of Lafayette's athletics grounds.

With the "grade in their favor," as *The Lehigh Burr* put it, the Brown and White would score in the first half on a 20 yard Warriner touchdown run, with Dashiell converting the kick. Before the end of the half, a fight broke out, started by Lehigh just before halftime, despite the Brown and White's 6-0 lead.

Lehigh's 1889 Football Team

But Lafayette in the second half would have the field and sun advantage, and would rally back after E.B. Camp's own 20 yard run after the break, and Francis March's kick tying the score.

The game would end in a 6-6 tie, called on account of darkness. Neither side was satisfied, but the Lehigh contingent was especially disappointed.

"Only the remarkable incompetency of the umpire prevented Lehigh winning," *The Lehigh Burr* said of the official from Princeton. "With his repeated declaration that Lehigh did no more fouling than their opponents, incontrovertible proof of his partiality is seen in his decisions. Ten fouls were given against Lehigh and but two against Lafayette. Indeed no sooner would our men force the ball close to Lafayette's goal line than his inevitable whistle would sound, and but for the fact that the only touchdown was made from about the twenty yard line, it is doubtful if we would have scored at all."

All that was left to determine the Championship of Pennsylvania was Lafayette's and Lehigh's return games against Penn. If Lehigh could beat Penn at home, the title would effectively be theirs, since they would have gone 1-0-1 against Lafayette.

The Brown and White would play on their slippery and wet field, due to recent rains, and shut out Penn 8-0 to capture the title, ending a dominating performance with a line plunge by Dashiell as the last play of the game.

The Lehigh Burr displayed the records of Lehigh, Lafayette and Penn in the Championship of Pennsylvania series in their December 1st edition, and the Lehigh team photo in 1889 also proudly displayed their homemade banner: "Champions of Pennsylvania."

They didn't display the cup commissioned by R.P. Linderman, however.

Shortly after Lehigh won the Championship of Pennsylvania, Penn publicly refused to play Lafayette again in football due to their violent behavior during their visit to Easton.

The Championship of Pennsylvania year of athletics had two lasting legacies for both teams.

For Lehigh, after winning the Championship, a wealthy alumnus, Rollin H. Wilbur, arranged for a private car and a train tour of the South in order for the Brown and White to play three schools below the Mason/Dixon line.

"The car was decorated on either side with strips of canvas bearing the legend: "The Lehigh University Football Team — Champions of Pennsylvania," *The Lehigh Burr* gushed while detailing their trip to Annapolis, Baltimore, Monticello, and Washington, DC, even taking in a production of *Richard III*.

On the field, the Brown and White roundly thrashed Navy, Johns Hopkins and Virginia, and the team came back to Bethlehem at 8:30 in the morning on the following Monday. "Three games were played on three successive days, scoring 102 points to their opponents 18, and involving nearly eight hundred miles of travel, *The Lehigh Burr* wrote, "and the team returned having added 'Champions of the South' to their other laurels."

After his playing days, Dashiell would be a successful coach at Navy, and a very influential member of Walter Camp's rules committee.

Dashiell's teammate, fullback Samuel Warriner, would become famous not for his post-graduate football career, but his post-graduate business career, as a mechanical engineer for a variety of coal companies.

He would rise to become president of the Lehigh Coal and Navigation Company, the most powerful force in the industry. It would be a position he would hold for 25 years.

But for Lafayette, Lehigh's success and rise in 1889 past their rivals caused something much more lasting.

"As the decade of the 1890s drew to a close," March wrote in *Athletics at Lafayette College*, "the football crowds grew in numbers and it became very evident to the friends of Lafayette that an enclosed field and a grandstand would be necessary if Lafayette were to hold their own with their favorite rivals. It seemed advisable for the undergraduates, who had up until this time run athletics by themselves without the assistance of the alumni or the interference of the faculty, to reorganize the [athletic] association in such a way as to bring to their assistance the body of loyal alumni who were already showing their interest in the new athletics."

At the close of 1889, Lafayette's modern athletics department was born.

8. LAFAYETTE REBUILDS A CONTENDER

Francis A. March Jr., was the son of Francis March Sr., the first chair of the English Language Department at Lafayette College.

March the senior, known as the inventor of modern academic English class instruction in both high schools and colleges, was the first-ever endowed chair of that discipline. He was also a big fan of the football team as well.

March the junior was as influential as his academic father, but in a different way.

As alumnus of Lafayette and avid fan of athletics, he embodied the college in a way few could top. His wedding to Alice Gray Youngman was the first such event ever held in Lafayette's on-campus chapel and the first "all-Lafayette wedding," according to David Bishop Skillman's *Biography of a College.*

March the junior, a Lafayette man through and through, entered the business of managing an athletic department at a time when collegiate athletics were largely run by the students themselves.

And by entering the business of running an athletic program, he oversaw a period of time that would witness Lafayette College become a national power in football.

He would also be a lifelong fan – one that left an indelible mark on the program.

After the disappointing end to the 1889 season, Lafayette had several large problems that required solving.

The first involved finances, something that must have been brought even more into focus by Lehigh's victory lap down South.

"At Lafayette, Spalding's bill for the equipment of the team was like the national debt, a sort of personal investment that was never fully paid," March wrote in his book *Athletics at Lafayette College*. Along with mandatory student dues for athletics, that were not always collected, "once in a while, when the Spalding bill would become too big, a bazaar would be held in the city of Easton," he wrote, "and the profits turned over to the athletic committee [to pay down the debt]."

What was frustrating to people like March was that he saw the potential of having paid attendance at the games fund athletics, but it required some infrastructure.

BEFORE THERE WERE GRANDSTANDS OR BLEACHERS

"As old Lafayette field was not enclosed," March wrote, "it was impossible to make all the spectators pay for the privilege of seeing the contests. The spectators sat on the ground or stood, and the dormitory rooms were used as reserved seats for young men and their sweethearts. It was notorious that anyone who desired could beat any scheme to pay without any great difficulty."

Such issues of finance were a scene that was playing out at other schools across the country, including Penn and Princeton. March, looking to these schools for answers, convinced the students at Lafayette that an alumni committee to handle the revenues, instead of students, would be a logical course of action.

The second problem for Lafayette involved scheduling.

In 1889, Lafayette's students had scheduled fourteen games for their team to play in a month and a half season. "Intercollegiate schedules which were arranged that were so long and difficult and involved so much travelling that they could not absorb the entire energy of the players," Skillman wrote in *The Biography of a College.*

Making scheduling even more challenging was the soured relations with Penn, stemming from the safety debacle from the Championship of Pennsylvania series against them that year.

Not playing Penn in football was a real detriment to Lafayette in terms of their ambitions to become a part of the Intercollegiate Football Association, an influential group that was establishing national rules for the game.

It also meant that Lafayette would have to continue to travel further and further to play games. Instead of an easy trip to Philadelphia, Lafayette would have to take costly weekend trips to Virginia to play football.

Restoring relations with Penn, therefore, would go a long way towards solving their scheduling problems.

The third issue involved reforming the reputation of Lafayette in the local area.

The bad publicity stemming from the "ruffianly mobs of Lafayette fans" fighting against the Penn players in 1889 stung, and part of that was attributed to the lack of organization of athletics, including the picking of team captains, training, and other matters of athletics. Able and willing alumni could help, and wanted to help, in all of these areas.

This also came at a time when the influential *Harpers Weekly* was starting to write about Lehigh's athletic experiences in a positive light in regards to the big issues surrounding college football at the time.

"It is well known that with the growing interest in athletics the tendency for marauding and carrying on after dark by the students has been on the decline," Malcolm W. Ford of *Harpers Weekly* wrote. "Such is the story as told by the representatives of Columbia, Princeton, University of Pennsylvania, Amherst, Williams, Lehigh and Swarthmore, and it shows that that so far athletics in these institutions are considered beneficial."

It could not have been taken very well on College Hill, Lafayette to be painted as the "ruffians" in comparison to the "gentlemen" of Lehigh.

By the end of 1889, less than a month after "losing" the Championship of Pennsylvania, Lafayette's students chose to allow for the alumni to form an advisory committee to "aid us in managing athletics," according to the group's charter, which was modelled after a similar one drafted at Princeton.

March, one of the founding members of the alumni group, wasted no time in addressing the problems.

"Representatives at once got in touch with the Pennsylvania athletic committee and re-established harmony with that institution," March wrote in *Athletics at Lafayette College*, "and enough money was raised to build a small grandstand which was erected in front of Martien Hall and held about 250 persons. Such a stand in our modern day would be little more than a joke, but it was greeted with great enthusiasm at Lafayette College."

The grandstand, with five tiny bleachers, made the contests more comfortable, especially for the ladies, but it couldn't initially improve the product on the field.

As Lafayette struggled to find its footing in 1890, Lehigh would lose to Penn twice, putting them out of the running for an unofficial championship of Pennsylvania.

Those frustrating losses to Penn would allow the Brown and White to focus on exacting their pound of flesh from Lafayette.

They would dominate the Maroon and White that season, exacting a 30-0 win in Easton and demolishing Lafayette 66-6 in South Bethlehem.

Up to that time, these were the two largest margins of victory at home and on the road in the Rivalry.

Lehigh's fullback George C. Hutchinson, named "Forked Lightning" for his speed and ability, dominated the Maroon and White with eight touchdowns in both games, including scoring "one touchdown by faking a punt," according to *Legends of Lehigh - Lafayette*.

"When the Brown and White bore off the victory with the score of 30 to 0," *The Lafayette* solemnly reported, "there was not a person among the thousand spectators who was not greatly surprised at the course of events."

Despite the large setbacks in 1890, there was optimism at Lafayette for the upcoming year, as people knew they were recruiting some strong players that would leap them back into contention.

They would also gain a very important fan.

Dr. Ethelbert D. Warfield

"On March 7th, 1891," March wrote in *Athletics at Lafayette College*, "Dr. Ethelbert D. Warfield was elected president of Lafayette College. Dr. Warfield was an athletic enthusiast and from the beginning of his distinguished service at Lafayette took an active interest in college athletics and a sympathetic interest in the work of the alumni advisory committee."

Athletic enthusiast might have been understating things.

A Princeton graduate, Warfield came to Lafayette from Miami of Ohio, where he not only founded the football team but also played on it, making him "probably the first president to incur an injury while playing on a college team," Ronald A. Smith mentioned in his book *Pay for Play: A History of Big-Time Athletic College Reform*.

Warfield felt football was a critical way to promote an institution of higher learning, and at Miami of Ohio had insisted that every man in the school try out for the team.

Lafayette still regarded itself, in some ways, as a school with its roots as a seminary. As a strong believer in Christian values, Dr. Warfield fit the bill perfectly, and he was a stirring leader for the school.

Football also fit very well in Dr. Warfield's philosophy of "muscular Christianity," which was to emphasize physical education (and sport) in order to develop young men's overall spiritual being. Football was an integral part of that mission in his mind.

But the seeds of his fateful decision to come to Lafayette may have been planted by a good friend at his alma mater.

"Once before as an undergraduate," David Bishop Skillman's *Biography of a College* wrote, "Dr. Warfield had come to Lafayette with a fellow student, Henry H. Wells, to visit a brother of the latter, Theodore L. Wells, '84."

It wasn't said whether they were visiting Lafayette to watch one of the first few football games on campus that Theodore, the founding father of Lafayette football, was busy arranging, or whether he was participating in football games as a referee, as Henry H. Wells did on several occasions. It seems likely that he was there in some measure to watch or participate in football activities, considering his later enthusiasm for the game.

What is certain is that as soon as Dr. Warfield became Lafayette's president, he was very active in matters of the football team, including going as far as helping set the fall schedule for the Maroon and White, working eagerly alongside the alumni association led by Francis March.

In 1891, March led the charge to adopt Phase II of his plan, involving the formation of a "scrub team," a squad that would serve as a way of identifying talent for the football team, as well as allowing them to perform full 11-on-11 practices.

The other major move March would make was to hire Lafayette's first football coach.

"It was the presence of Mr. [Paul] Dashiell at Lehigh that induced the present writer, during the winter of 1891, to pass around the hat among the Lafayette alumni for funds to be used in employing a coach for Lafayette," March admitted in *Athletics at Lafayette College*.

Wallace S. Moyle, who came from Yale, played end on some of the best teams in the country from 1888 to 1891 as a substitute. Shortly after graduation, he was hired by March to coach the Maroon and White football team. Like Dashiell, he was expected to be head coach and star player.

Further helping matters was the resumption of the Championship of Pennsylvania series in 1891 - with a twist.

In addition to the home-and-home series with Penn, Lehigh and Lafayette allowed their teams to face off against each other one extra time that season in Wilkes-Barre, the only neutral-site game ever played up to that point.

"The football management deserves much praise for what it has done this year," *The Lafayette* said in regards to the Wilkes-Barre contest in 1891, which they called an exhibition game. "The management has been under much heavier expense this year than usual...the trainer had to be paid, many of the scrubs had suits furnished to them, without which they would not have had the necessary training. This third game with Lehigh will help to make up the additional expense of the year, besides giving the students a chance to see a game between Lafayette and Lehigh on neutral ground, a thing often wished for by many."

By 1891, Lehigh had fallen a little from their Championship of Pennsylvania team, though they had more than enough to sweep the struggling Maroon and White, 22-4 (in Bethlehem) and 6-2 (in Easton), before contesting the final "exhibition" in Wilkes-Barre.

The C.R.R.N.J. railroad, a competitor of the Packer family's Lehigh Valley Railroad, provided a train for the Lafayette students and friends to head up to Wilkes-Barre, "furnishing special rates of $2.25 for those who wished to witness the game," *The Lafayette* reported. Perhaps not unexpectedly, the Lehigh contingent took the Lehigh Valley Road instead.

A crowd of over 5,000 fans, "by far the largest crowd that ever witnessed a football game in Wilkes-Barre," attended the matchup, with "half a dozen big busses holding crowds and a large number of private carriages, containing many of Wilkes-Barre's fair ones," *The Lafayette* said. Most of the crowd cheered on Lafayette, including the boys of nearby Wyoming Seminary. "The cheering of the students seemed to startle the natives," according to *The Lafayette*.

Lehigh would win against heavily injured Lafayette 16-2 in an "intercollegiate championship game," according to *The Pittsburg Dispatch* that was "scientifically played on a poor field," the field in this case being muddy West Side Park.

Lafayette's only points would come early, when Lehigh was tackled for a safety, before the Brown and White scored three straight touchdowns to come away with the win.

(It would be a year after this game that Mansfield and Wyoming Seminary would play what was considered the first-ever night football game at the Great Mansfield fairgrounds nearby, powered by light bulbs and electricity from Thomas Edison's General Electric Company.)

Despite the three-game sweep in 1891, Lafayette was optimistic that they were making strides to improve their program greatly over the coming years.

"We are glad to announce that Mr. W.S. Moyle, our foot-ball trainer, is again with us," *The Lafayette* said the following year. "His work with the team last year was very encouraging, and under his direction we hope for still better things during the present season. Mr. Moyle meets with a warm welcome and can depend upon harty (sic) co-operation."

The students running Lehigh's athletic department must have noticed as well, for Josh Hartwell, who was a teammate of Moyle's at Yale, became the Brown and White's next player/coach.

Lehigh had a budding national reputation to uphold, too, as the team was noticed by papers like *The New York Times*.

"The football team received several setbacks this week," they reported in 1892 under the headline 'Lehigh Loses Two Teeth'. "Pellet has [transferred] to Cornell, where he will probably play half back. Brisco, [transfer] from Johns Hopkins, hurt his knee so badly in practice that he had to be taken to the hospital and will not play any more this year. Van Cleve has had a couple of his teeth knocked out, and Faust, the plucky half-back, has had his shoulder knocked out of place."

The 1892 season would be a disappointment for Lehigh, with their rash of injuries resulting in a six-game losing streak, including a 4-0 loss to Lafayette in Easton where the Maroon and White, behind their own version of the V formation, plowed through Lehigh's line to score the only touchdown. "The attendance at the game was large," *The Lafayette* reported. "The day was a cold one, and the number of carriages was not so large as usual. The halls facing the campus were unusually well patronized. The students were jubilant over the game, and a large delegation paraded the town afterward."

But the Brown and White would get their revenge later that year in Bethlehem, winning 15-6 in a game that was "a clean one throughout," according to *The Lafayette*. "Personalities and slugging, two things which are always apt to crop out in a Lehigh-Lafayette game, were in minus quantities. When time was called, the two teams were swallowed up in the mass of people, many jubilant and with stuffed pocket-books, others dejected and with only their railroad tickets in their purses."

The epic fights between the schools' players and fans were already becoming legendary, but according to student paper accounts, gambling was also very much a part of the games as well.

It was 1893, though, where Lehigh's fortunes would be at once successful and disastrous.

It was common knowledge in 1893 that Lehigh was a rich institution.

"[Our] forced economy in itself is a great hindrance to our success in athletic competitions," a 1890s letter sent out by Lafayette's alumni committee said. "Our nearest antagonists - Lehigh, Princeton, Pennsylvania - are now so wealthy, that we, with our comparatively untrained teams, are at great disadvantage. Our alumni all desire our success but few realize how much this success depends on them."

Thanks in no small part to Asa Packer's bequest to Lehigh of a huge sum of money and stock after his death in 1879, the University was the richest institution of higher learning at the time, surpassing, according to *The New York Times*, even Harvard and Yale.

By the order of Asa Packer's will, a significant number of the assets of the University were actual shares of Lehigh Valley Railroad stock.

The vastness of Lehigh's endowment was controversial, especially when

Lafayette College could have also used a monetary gift from Packer.

"In one view, the gift is the noblest one of the kind ever made," *The New York Times* said of the bequest, "for it establishes the only institution - so far as we know - which gives absolutely free tuition to all comers, rich or poor."

"It is merely in an economic sense," the article continues, "that the opinion is expressed that any addition to the more than 300 colleges now dwarfing and starving one another in this country is a wicked waste of resources."

For more than a decade, Packer's success in building the railway and navigating the business dealings of the railroad barons kept his family (and Lehigh University) rich, even a decade after his death.

But in 1893 things would begin to change.

The L.V.R.R. stock was of great benefit to Lehigh - as long as the stock price remained high. This would not last.

In 1893, the entire American financial system went from boom times to crisis.

A series of failed investment endeavors by the banks, fuelled by massive lending, led to a rash of bank defaults and closures. A silver mine boom, and subsequent protectionism scheme, ended up undermining the gold standard upon which the banks' legitimacy was based, causing investments to flee the country.

The money used to finance the railroad company expansion suddenly dried up. When the Reading Railroad declared bankruptcy, outside investors looked closely at the source of the Packer fortune, the Lehigh Valley Railroad, to see if they would be the next victims.

Unemployment in Pennsylvania skyrocketed, affecting many Lehigh and Lafayette graduates. By the end of 1893, railroad strikes were plaguing the L.V.R.R. and there was great uncertainty in its ability to survive the crisis.

Several prominent train crashes involving the L.V.R.R. were national news, which didn't help.

Over the course of 1893, the richest university in the country would go through the first true financial struggle of its existence.

Lehigh's 1893 Football Team

"When the panic of 1857 came," E.B. Coxe, Asa Packer's one-time business partner and large L.V.R.R. stockholder said in a commencement speech at Lehigh, "[Asa] stood as firm as a rock and fought to win, and he did. That is what we have to do today with Lehigh University. She has struck a panic, but she is not going to waver. Her resources may not be as great as they were, but her diploma is going to be as great in value as it ever was."

During this time, Lehigh's nationally-recognized football program provided a welcome distraction from the seriousness all around them, even though football games, in general, were becoming much more violent and dangerous. This was, in part, due to the mass-momentum plays (like the "Lehigh V") that were revolutionized by Lehigh and starting to be used ever more effectively by Lafayette.

Athletes like halfback Godwin Ordway and end Walter Okeson, with mops of long hair to protect their heads from concussion and injury due to the onslaught of mass momentum plays, were stars.

Okeson was an ironman who starred on both offense and defense and understood the game of football completely. He would not miss a game from 1893 through the rest of his Lehigh playing career.

Lehigh's 1893 schedule was a first for the Brown and White, packed with high-profile opponents of the time.

The matchups with national championship contender Princeton were of particular interest.

Back in 1891, Lehigh's star center, 24 year old D.M. Balliet, became Lehigh's first-ever Walter Camp All-American. But in 1892, the 25 year old Balliet enrolled at nearby Princeton, where he helped the Tigers win several more national titles and continued his all-American ways.

Even though he remained friendly with his former teammates, he nonetheless suited up against them, twice beating Lehigh 12-0 and 28-6. Balliet would go on to become a big part of Princeton's undefeated national championship team of 1893.

Lehigh Center D.M. Balliet

While there was no rule preventing this type of player transfer, nor a rule preventing a team from suiting up a 25 or 26 year old player, many schools were finally pushing back against these types of practices, enforcing the idea of only suiting up players who were current students with good academic standing.

Balliet was in the center of the controversy.

Princeton was roundly criticized for prying Balliet away from Lehigh.

In prior years, the press thought the Tigers had talked a good game in regards to actual students competing on their football teams. The presence of Balliet, however, made it seem like Princeton was not beyond enrolling mercenaries to win football games when it suited the school.

It was a big enough crisis to cause all the members of the old, powerful Intercollegiate Football Association to withdraw, and the existing college football governing order to collapse, just like many banks were at the time.

Despite the turmoil – and the lack of their former star player – Lehigh's football team did very well in 1893.

Their early losses came to Penn and Princeton, who were both loaded with these questionable players. As such, the defeats were not seen by the fans as much of a blemish on their record. The Brown and White scored more than 4 points on Princeton, which was encouraging to them. (They would be the only team that scored more than four points on Princeton all season.)

From there Lehigh would defeat the other national powerhouses on their schedule.

Against Army, Lehigh benefitted from some injuries on the Cadet team to cruise to an 18-0 victory – including a broken ankle on the Cadet's starting halfback, undoubtedly caused by a mass momentum play.

After the season, Army's superintendent was very critical of football's benefit to the officer corps.

"It is doubtful, in my opinion," Major O.H. Harvey said in a quote in *The New York Times*, "if the benefits from playing this game are commensurate with the risks it entails to life and limb, which, according to statistics, are much greater than commonly supposed."

Against Cornell, Lehigh would win 14-0 after denying them three times at their goal line. In the game Lehigh would face Cornell's version of the "Flying Wedge," a new mass momentum play devised by Harvard's head coach, but it wasn't enough to allow the Big Red to score any points against the Brown and White.

Against Navy, Lehigh would fall behind 6-0 in Annapolis before roaring back to score 12 unanswered points to win the contest. "Lehigh forced the fight in the second half and played their stratagems to good effect," *The New York Times* reported, showing that, nationally, Lehigh was seen as a team that could engineer wins out of their plays over bigger brawn.

Using interference and misdirection, Balliet's innovation, Lehigh continued to beat bigger, more powerful teams.

Lehigh also swept their nearby Eastonian rivals as well.

In the first game, after falling behind 6-0, Ordway and Lehigh's strong line would ultimately wear down Lafayette's defensive front, eventually piling up a 22-6 win.

In the second game, "although the threatened, inclemency of the weather kept many would-be spectators from the game," *The Lafayette* reported, "the crowd was the largest ever to our campus to witness a foot-ball contest. It was unusually exciting and the victory was a matter of speculation until the close of the game, for the score stood 4-0, Lehigh having scored on a fluke, until five minutes before time was called, when Lehigh made her second touchdown."

The 10-0 win would not be the end of Lehigh's football season, however.

"Considerable interest is being manifested in Southern college circles in the football game to be played at Manhattan Field next Saturday between the teams of the University of North Carolina and Lehigh," *The New York Times* reported the last week in November. "It will be the first time that a Southern team has ever played a football eleven in the North. They all seem to regard the University of North Carolina as their champion to test their strength against a good Northern team."

The game would also be Lehigh's first-ever contest in New York City, taking place at Manhattan Field next to the Polo Grounds. (Lafayette had already faced off against Columbia in the Big Apple in 1889.)

Though some media members predicted a bigger, stronger Tar Heel side being able to dominate Lehigh physically, the Brown and White instead used their "science," as *The New York Times* called it, in a 34-0 romp over the best team in the South.

Manhattan Field (Polo Grounds)

"A large delegation from Bethlehem and members of the Lehigh Club, of this city," *The New York Herald* reported, "occupied one of the stands, freely bedecked with brown and white."

"'Hoo, 'roo, 'ray! Hoo, 'roo, ray! Ray, 'ray, 'ray! Lehigh!' was heard, and the Pennsylvanians appeared," *The New York Times* reported. "The Lehighs would play a trick or two, old ones at that, and in the end win by 34 to 0."

Thanks to their first-ever win in New York City over the consensus "Champions of the South," Lehigh's successful 1893 came at the right time for the University. They raised the name of Lehigh at a time when the school was undergoing some major challenges.

Lafayette fans were not sitting idly by, though, as Lehigh's successes continued to mount at the expense of the Maroon and White. Francis March had a plan to improve, and they were sticking to it, with the hope that it would pay off down the line.

It would.

1894 was a tough year for both Lehigh and Lafayette for different reasons.

For Lafayette, a large athletics spending deficit was being put right by the Maroon and White's first athletic director, Francis A. March. His plan, to enclose Lafayette's field in order to charge admission to the games to make athletics self-sustaining, was proceeding only with the largesse of interested Lafayette alumni who wanted to see a good football team. Though still largely run by students, the alumni fundraising and leadership were putting much in order.

But for Lehigh, the limitations of a student-run athletic department were becoming very apparent. Perhaps tied to the financial crisis involving the school, the Brown and White's athletic debt was skyrocketing, starting alumni cries that they should be "helping" and running the finances of the athletic department, just like Lafayette.

Lehigh students were not only unable to collect athletic dues from all the students, the mismanagement had caused a deficit in regards to owed funds. Creditors were demanding payment, forcing Lehigh's alumni association and board of trustees to step in and manage the day-to-day affairs of athletics.

Additionally, it meant Lehigh would have a fourteen game schedule in 1894, set up by the students, while Lafayette's eleven game schedule would be set up by the board of trustees and the faculty.

This would affect that year's Rivalry games in a positive way for Lafayette.

Three weeks prior to the first game at Easton, Lehigh would play five grueling games against powerhouse teams: the semi-professional Orange (NJ) Athletic Club, Princeton, Yale, Navy, and also, for good measure, a scheduled rematch against North Carolina at Lehigh's athletic grounds.

Perhaps with a more level head to health and academics, Lafayette scheduled only two games over that same stretch: Penn and the Orange (NJ) Athletic Club.

At Lafayette's newly enclosed field, the Maroon and White would christen the playing surface, called March Field, in style.

"The clouds were hanging low, the wind was sweeping across the field, when the gates opened on the afternoon of the 14th," *The Lafayette* proclaimed. "Soon groups of students might be seen walking across the campus to the field; later, they become more frequent, and a steady line is entering the gate. The east bleachers were filled long before the game, and when the Lehigh delegation ascended the hill, they had to content themselves with the south mass of seats. The field looked, indeed, beautiful. The Lafayette seats surmounted by a large banner of the glorious colors, bunting drawn to sides; the students and the ribbons and banners flaunting gallantly in the breeze."

Lafayette would win resoundingly 28-0, thanks to the emergence of a strong new eighteen year old sophomore halfback called George Barclay, who would score three touchdowns and kick all of the extra points.

"Their players were in the pink of condition," the new Lehigh student newspaper, *The Brown and White*, reported, "having carefully trained and rested for several weeks, while our men were in a badly used up state. This is our second defeat by Lafayette in several years and its novelty no doubt lends a spice to the game in the eyes of the Easton men. However, we were outplayed start to finish."

Lafayette's March Field, c. 1898

Though Lehigh would beat them a couple of weeks later 11-8, coming from behind to score a late touchdown to escape South Bethlehem with a series split, enthusiasm was high for Maroon and White football.

"The college is under obligations to Alumni who, by their valuable suggestion and example, have aided very materially in bringing the foot-ball team up to its present standard," *The Lafayette* said that year. "Mr. G.K. Voigt, '94, is particularly deserving of thanks for his generous sacrifice of valuable time to the team, and for his valuable assistance in coaching, preliminary to the Lehigh game. Such manifest interest on the part of Alumni cannot fail to inspire the team with greater desire for brilliant play and zealous training."

One particular alumnus was their great early athlete, Jacob D. Updegrove, who would found Lafayette's pre-med program, arranging their first biology class as the "Director of Physical Training and Lecturer on

Hygiene." His program, which allowed for admittance to Penn's medical program after four years of college, had the effect of attracting new football recruits.

In 1895, Lafayette's debts were now starting to be paid down just as the extent of Lehigh's financial mess was becoming apparent. This gave Lafayette the opportunity to grow its football program further, which is exactly what Lafayette president Ethelbert Warfield did.

Warfield's most momentous decision regarding the football program was to hire a new young coach named Parke H. Davis.

Davis was different than most other coaches of that time in that he was not also a playing coach.

Parke H. Davis

He was called Lafayette's first "athletic trainer" by David Bishop Skillman in *The Biography of a College*.

"He was not like W.S. Moyle," Skillman said of the coach who Parke H. Davis replaced. "The latter had not only coached, but had played fullback on the team. He [Moyle] lost his popularity and his job because he carried the ball himself on nearly every play."

Davis, a former lineman at Princeton, came to Lafayette from Amherst, noted *Legends of Lehigh - Lafayette*. Davis didn't come to hog the ball, but instead was a well-connected coach who had rubbed elbows with some powerful men. At Princeton, he worked with instrumental alumnus (and avid football fan) Woodrow Wilson. At Amherst, he would work with a student-manager named Calvin Coolidge.

Paid the princely sum of $1,200 a year, Davis was worth every penny to Lafayette as they climbed back into the national sporting ranks. In many ways he was the template of the modern football coach.

As coach of football, baseball, and track, he developed a year-round training table for his athletes, most notably George O. Barclay, who would excel at all three sports. But Davis' true genius came from his ability to motivate his football team to new heights.

"It has often been said that if Lehigh's team wore any other letter than L. on their breasts we would defeat them more frequently," *The Lafayette* stated in the middle of one of their long losing streaks to the Brown and

White. "Gentlemen of the eleven, it is your duty to knock that aphorism into a cocked hat. You can and will prove to us in the coming game that you can defeat Lehigh, if they are even covered with the traditional brown and white and enclosed with a multitude of L's."

Davis believed that, with his system of training in place, all that was needed to push Lafayette over the top was motivation and belief in themselves.

In 1895, the system was starting to work.

Similar to the prior year, Lafayette made sure that there was plenty of time for rest and recovery before the Maroon and White's first game against Lehigh, allowing for an easy game versus Rutgers first, then ten days of rest.

The softer schedule meant young Lafayette was well rested for Lehigh, who had played a grueling schedule (including Navy) seven days before their first game vs. Lafayette.

Both sides were focused on the fact that Lafayette had not beaten Lehigh on their home field in more than eight years.

"Everything else in our College world dwindles into insignificance beside the game to be played tomorrow," *The Lafayette* reported. "This is the important game of the year, this is the goal to which all eves have been turned for the last two months. We have gone up there before with strong teams and for apparently no other reason than that the team was rattled, we have been defeated. On you, the members of the team, there is the opportunity of beating Lehigh on her own grounds. The Brown and White is stirring their men up and are calling forth songs, and be assured their enthusiasm will be at flood tide. Let ours not be a whit less, but let us drown out their songs by our yells and have only one aim—Victory For Lafayette."

"It is the game of the year that we must win," *The Brown and White* countered. "It is Lehigh's proud boast that she had not been defeated by Lafayette on her own grounds for eight years and we must keep that worthy record up. The balance of power seems to lie in the cheering, and we hope it can never be said that a Lehigh team failed to win the day because they were not sufficiently encouraged by the support of the University."

The game was well attended by fans of both schools. The mob in front of the ticket office was so large that Lehigh needed to bring extra men outside to allow people to buy their tickets.

"The special train that left the L.V.R.R. station at 1:30 Saturday afternoon for Bethlehem," *The Lafayette* reported, "had on board Captain Boericke and his men, under the care of Manager Nesbit and Coach Davis, the 'one hundred lustily lunged howlers,' the rest of the student body, and three hundred or more townsmen."

The crowd filed in more than an hour before kickoff and Lehigh's bleachers were packed well before the start of the game. Lafayette's style was to be more physical than Lehigh, smashing holes up the middle for their talented halfbacks Barclay and Walbridge. They succeeded masterfully, jumping to a 16-0 halftime lead.

"During the intermission of ten minutes which followed, the Lehigh bleachers sang 'Lehigh always wins in the second half,' but it was a half-hearted song," *The Lafayette* reported. "However, their team braced up wonderfully during the breathing spell and by some hard work succeeded in scoring twelve points during the second half."

Lehigh did play better in the second half, outscoring the Maroon and White, but it wasn't nearly enough, falling 22-12, allowing Lafayette to celebrate on Lehigh Field for the first time in eight years.

"When the train pulled out of Bethlehem in the evening for the trip home," *The Lafayette* said, "enthusiasm could in no way express their condition; it rather bordered on the delirious. Students hugged each other like bears, they sang songs and even the most dignified citizens could not refrain from whooping occasionally. They had been journeying to Bethlehem for seven years, to return each time with fallen crests at the defeat of their favorite college, but at last victory had perched on Lafayette's standards and the maroon and white was flaunted wildly in the breezes."

The Lafayette's student editor couldn't have been more delighted.

"Seven editors have passed from this position without having had such a delightful task," he wrote. "Team after team has gone up there— and those too that have coped with strong college teams better than Lehigh's— and have been beaten apparently for no other reason than that it had become an established custom to be beaten on those grounds. But now that custom is annihilated, and this year's team has established a precedent which it will be well for future teams to follow."

A week later, in Easton, alumni flocked to see Lafayette defeat Lehigh again, this time by a 14-6 margin, capping a 6-2 record and the most successful season in years. Similar to the prior game, the Maroon and White leapt to a 14-0 lead in the first half, and Lehigh's comeback was not enough.

The Lafayette's student editor reflected on their successful season.

"Two Victories over Lehigh in one year," he wrote. "Only a Lafayette man can realize all that there is in these words. Only a Lafayette man can rejoice to the fullest extent at such results. They are full of meaning to him as he thinks how many times we have contended with our up-the-river rivals and have been beaten apparently without cause. But now our luck has changed and this is only the beginning of what we shall do."

As successful as that season was, it would pale in comparison to the success of the following year.

The only problem was it would come at the cost of not playing against their hated Rivals.

"The season of 1895 ended in a burst of glory," Parke H. Davis contributed for *Athletics at Lafayette College*. "Lafayette was a real football power."

9. THE YEAR OF 1896

By the late 1800s, the Rivalry had already started to take on a unique flavor not only with the players, but with the fans.

Games between Harvard, Princeton and Yale were big events between schools that considered themselves rivals, but those games took place at neutral grounds, like New York City or Springfield, Mass, and could only be pulled together once a year. Events like that were grand, but the fans could only schedule a major rail trip once a year to see their team play.

But Lehigh and Lafayette's proximity and rail connection meant both schools could schedule each other twice a season. No overnight trip was necessary - twice a year, by nightfall, one school was victorious and able to celebrate in their home town.

In 1896, Parke H. Davis did what many thought was not possible by guiding Lafayette to the top of the college football world.

But it came at a price.

Chambersburg, PA is located nearly 150 miles from Easton, PA. It is the home of one of oldest semi-pro baseball teams in existence, the Chambersburg Maroons.

In the first year of the Maroons' existence as a member of the Cumberland Valley League, in the summer of 1895, they won the league championship. In their second year, the Maroons were loaded again, with a roster that included six players who would go on to play in the major leagues.

Lafayette's star halfback, George O. Barclay, took two train trips from Easton to Chambersburg and played baseball for them over the summer of 1896.

He was provided two round-trip train tickets, equipment, room and board, and expenses for his services rendered as a baseball player.

Chambersburg Maroons Team Picture, 1895

The 20 year old Barclay was not the only college athlete of his time to play baseball over the summer with professional teams. In the era before there were formalized rules of eligibility, playing baseball over the summer was something that was not strictly amateur in terms of the British definition. In a world where teachers and coaches played on the intercollegiate teams and players who were 25 years old were tolerated, a player would not be disqualified from competition because of summer baseball.

"Prior to the two football games in 1896," Courtney Michelle-Smith's dissertation *A Delicate Balance: An Examination of Lehigh's Athletic Culture and Athletic Extra-Curriculum* writes, "representatives from the Lehigh and Lafayette athletic committees decided to write uniform eligibility guidelines for the first time in the Rivalry's history."

Those guidelines, cleared by the faculties of both schools, required that the players be bona fide students, not receive any financial aid for attending the schools, and, most importantly, not play sports "for a financial consideration." The list of participants were to be compiled and submitted to faculty representatives at both schools to endorse.

Such an act was deemed necessary by both schools for several reasons.

First, intercollegiate football did not have an official rule-making body like the NCAA to enforce eligibility standards, so as was becoming the custom of the time, Lehigh and Lafayette took matters in their own hands to come up with rules on who should play college football.

Second, standards for participation were coming under more scrutiny as it was becoming increasingly clear that the top schools in the Ivy League and elsewhere were suiting up college representatives in name only. At Lehigh and Lafayette, it was an important matter of pride that they did things differently.

Schools like Bucknell were publicly declaring that their teams would only comprise true student-athletes, and not "professionals," and Lehigh and Lafayette believed in this as well.

As Lehigh and Lafayette's football seasons in 1896 progressed, they went in two different directions.

The Brown and White played a tough schedule against no less than three national contenders, and lost all three.

Penn, in the middle of the longest winning streak in the nation, easily handled Lehigh 34-0. Princeton, always in the mix for a mythical national championship, defeated the Brown and White 16-0.

Lehigh also made a trip to Detroit, to highlight their brand of Eastern football in front of fans of one of the budding football powers of the Midwest, the University of Michigan.

(The undefeated Wolverines would overpower Lehigh 40-0, and would nearly end the 1896 season undefeated as well. Had they not fallen on the last day of the college football season 7-6 to the University of Chicago, who was coached by Hall-of-Famer Amos Alonzo Stagg, they might have been crowned the mythical national champions.)

Lehigh's record was 1-5, but Davis' Lafayette squad did not lose a single game over that stretch.

Their team had a young star hitting his prime, halfback George O. "Rose" Barclay, who was featured alongside 22 year old senior captain George Walbridge in the Maroon and White's rushing attack.

Aside from being a superlative athlete, Barclay is credited with inventing the first-ever football helmet in 1894, a series of leather straps worn by him over his head. It was supposed to prevent a common problem with football players called "cauliflower ears." The helmet covered the ears to prevent this from happening.

The first football helmet was "made by an Easton saddle maker from harness padding and rivets," *Legends of Lehigh - Lafayette* tells us. "Barclay, who was nicknamed 'Rose' because of his good looks and keen eye for the ladies, chose to take abuse for his invention in return for protecting his tender ears and pretty mug."

"Walbridge was the captain and the backfield work was largely built around him," Davis recalled to March in *Athletics at Lafayette College*. "He and Barclay made the best pair of backs Lafayette has ever known."

Lafayette had never beaten Princeton in their history, so when they tied the Tigers 0-0 in a rare home game against them, the growing number of Lafayette fans felt like it could be a very special season.

Lafayette fans knew that their team had a solid offense, but it was their stingy defense holding Princeton scoreless that really got the fan base excited.

George O. "Rose" Barclay

The Maroon and White then travelled south to play three games against the University of West Virginia over a long weekend.

Lafayette would be the first "major college" team from the East to play the Mountaineers, and it showed, with the Maroon and White outscoring West Virginia by a combined score of 58-0.

"The crowd of 2000 spectators never saw a game of foot-ball before and it was with great difficulty that they were kept off the field," *The Lafayette* reported. "After the game at Wheeling [West Virginia] 'Pop' Smith gave a reception and dance to the boys at Martin's Ferry, which was hugely enjoyed by all."

In the final game, a former Princeton player, Thomas Trenchard, suited up for the Mountaineers "to stem the tide, but to no avail," David Bishop Skillman noted in *The Biography of a College*. "The eligibility rules were such that the substitution passed without comment."

West Virginia had one very good player, tackle "Fieldling" Yost, who impressed team manager Storrs M. Bishop so much that he convinced him to accompany Lafayette's team back on the train to Easton to play against

Penn. Just in time, Yost was able to suit up against one of the most dominant teams in the country.

"[Yost] was permitted, on college comity, to recite in the freshman class," Skillman wrote. "Early in November he decided to return to the University of West Virginia. Writing from there, he said that 'next year I shall return and study at Lafayette, at least three years, as I informed you when I left' - an intention that was never carried out."

Since Penn competed in those Championship of Pennsylvania games with Lehigh and Lafayette, they had evolved into a national power. In the span of six years, Penn had not lost to a "small college" team, only suffering losses to Harvard, Yale, and Princeton.

Going into the game, Penn's team, who had head coach/player George Washington Woodruff as one of its stars, had not lost a game in two seasons, winning mythical national championships in 1894 and 1895 with 12-0 and 14-0 records, respectively. Penn was riding a 34 game winning streak into their game against Lafayette.

Their matchup with the Maroon and White almost didn't happen because a financial dispute about guarantees that required Francis A. March to intervene.

Football games became a financial windfall for Penn. Their brand-new state-of-the-art enclosed stadium, called Franklin Field, brought in more spectators and more money in the form of ticket revenue.

As was beginning to become the custom, home teams provided the opposing team a cut of the earnings of the games. In the case of Penn, when they negotiated with Lafayette's student leaders to pay them a paltry guarantee of $150, Lafayette alumni were in an uproar.

With Penn's take in tickets being well over $10,000, Lafayette alumni felt the student managers were fleeced.

A battle ensued between the Easton and Philadelphia papers over it, ending in Lafayette refusing to play Penn in 1895 under this arrangement.

It was only with March's intervention and expert negotiation that allowed the game with Penn to happen at all in 1896. It was made final on the campus of Pennsylvania, on October 17th, while Penn was beating Lehigh, 34-0.

"With this intercollegiate squabble the rivalry between the two institutions had become intense and when the game was played on the following Saturday there was an enormous crowd and each team was out for blood," March wrote in his book *Athletics at Lafayette College.*

Lafayette's chances for victory took another major hit on the day of the game.

"Halfway to Philadelphia on the train Captain Walbridge, on whom so much depended, was attacked by acute appendicitis," March wrote. "It was necessary to have the train met by an ambulance which took him to the hotel for medical examination. It was decided that he must submit at once to an operation."

Lafayette had no choice but to try to break Penn's 32 game winning streak without their captain - the man around whom the offense was based.

"Before taking the coach to the Pennsylvania field," March continued, "the team gathered in the room of their captain, who was to be taken that afternoon to the hospital, and listened to what he had to say. Others also spoke, and when the team left that room they were as determined a body as ever played for Lafayette."

Halfback and Captain George Walbridge, left, guard Charles "Babe" Rinehart, right

"With tears streaming down his cheeks," Skillman adds, "[Walbridge] gave the last instructions and exhortation. Under this spell the inspired players went to Franklin Field."

Walbridge's back-up, junior Harry Zeizer, suited up in his captains' place and played the game of his life.

By March's account, Penn was over-confident as they played Lafayette in front of a packed house of 13,000.

"On the side-lines a portly Philadelphia policeman told the writer that he hoped Lafayette would win," March wrote in *Athletics at Lafayette College*. "'These Pennsylvania kids are too cocky,' he said, and he was probably representative of a lively Philadelphia opinion."

Woodruff, Penn's coach and captain, inserted himself as the starting fullback, seeming to indicate that he was trying an experimental formation.

The first half favored Penn, who had a stiff wind at their backs. The Quakers (as Penn's team was called) threatened Lafayette's goal several times early on, but the Maroon and White held strong against Penn's attack and forced several fumbles to keep the game scoreless.

"Finally they succeeded in holding the ball," *The New York Times* reported, "and Uffenheimer was pushed through the centre [sic] for a touchdown. The kick-cut was a failure, and no more scoring was done in the half."

By the scoring method of the time, it was Penn 4, Lafayette 0 at halftime.

Lafayette continued their spirited play in the second half when the slightest of openings came up for the Maroon and White.

"As time went on it became plain that Lafayette was outplaying Penn," March wrote in *Athletics at Lafayette College*. "The ball was forced up the field again and again [in Penn's territory], and Penn, put on the defensive, was kicking. It was one of those kicks which opened the way for Lafayette's victory. Unable to gain, Minds of Pennsylvania was forced to kick hurriedly. The kick was blocked by Wiedenmeyer of Lafayette, Worthington falling on the ball on the University's 35 yard line."

Lafayette at Penn, October 23rd, 1896

"While Bray's kicking [for Lafayette] was not good," *The New York Times* adds, "the exhibition Mindes [sic] was giving was harrowing to the followers of Pennsylvania. Mindes kicked, and the ball rolled along the ground for a few yards and Lafayette got it."

With Lafayette's captain in the hospital, his life in danger undergoing surgery to remove his ruptured appendix, it was his teammate, Barclay that sealed the upset with plays that were likely designed for his captain and teammate.

"Bray dropped back as if about to kick," March describes in *Athletics at*

Lafayette College, "but the ball was passed to Barclay who dashed against the right side of the Pennsylvania line, was thrown, jumped to his feet again and rounding Pennsylvania's right end took the ball for a 20 yard run, being forced out of bounds on Pennsylvania's 5 yard line."

Moments later, with little time remaining, Barclay went around the left end for the touchdown - Yost's side on the offensive line – tying the game. Barclay then "easily kicked a goal," according to *The New York Times*, making the score Lafayette 6, Penn 4.

"The Quakers seemed stunned by the suddenness of the thing," *The New York Times* continued, "and for the short remaining time played like wooden men."

"Receiving a kickoff," March wrote in *Athletics at Lafayette College*, "Lafayette rushed the big University right down the field and time was called with the ball on Pennsylvania's 15 yard line with the ball in Lafayette's hands. The great game was over and Lafayette had won."

Scenes from the Lafayette students who made the trip, as well as some local Philadelphians who adopted the Maroon and White during the game, were of ecstasy.

"A procession was formed that seemed to include all of Lafayette and most of Easton," March recalled, "and as it marched down Chestnut Street singing its song of triumph, 'What's the score, six to four, Pennsylvania on the floor!', handkerchiefs were waved from the sidewalk and from windows which showed the sympathy of Philadelphia."

While delirious fans were triumphantly marching through Philadelphia, Walbridge's teammates returned to his hospital room, where, according to March, they sang the Doxology, "Praise God From Whom All Blessings Flow" along with him.

"In the evening," March continued, "the boys took possession of one of the Philadelphia theaters, the team in the boxes, the rooters in the gallery. Between acts the cheering was continuous and after Lafayette had exhausted itself college cheers for Lafayette were given by representatives of a dozen other colleges whose alumni had been present at the game."

Conversely, there was "no balm in Gilead for Pennsylvania to take the sting out of its defeat," *The New York Times* reported, "as it was directly due to their own bad playing." Additionally, Pennsylvania begged Lafayette's management for a rematch - this time, however, for 500 times the original guarantee or $7,500. "Lafayette wisely declined," Skillman wrote.

The celebrations continued when the trains arrived back at Easton.

"The various halls bordering the campus were decorated in fine style," *The Lafayette* wrote. "Banners were hung beneath the windows, streamers flaunted in the air, while the walls were for the most part covered in Chinese lanterns. At eight o' clock the students formed a line in front of McKeen and headed by the Triple City band, marched from the hill through the principal streets of the city amidst a blaze of red light, and the whiz and flash of fireworks."

A huge celebration, highlighted by students, rang through the streets of the town and had others wondering what was next for their triumphant team. Some students made a flaming version of the final score, "6-4," out of sawdust and kerosene.

Escorting a Victorious Team from the Station

"For the future this victory means that Lafayette will defeat Lehigh as never before," the student paper said. "It means that she will, in all probability, close the season with but four points against her."

The row that forced the 1896 Rivalry games to be cancelled illustrates how the Rivalry passions of both schools caused it to happen.

As per the agreement in April, both lists of players were given to each others' faculty to endorse for the upcoming games.

Lehigh, led by their English professor Charles L. Thornburg, challenged the eligibility of Lafayette's three strongest players: Barclay, Walbridge, and Bray.

"Angry Lafayette officials countered by challenging the eligibility of two Lehigh players," Michele-Smith said in *A Delicate Balance: An Examination of Lehigh University's Athletic Culture and Athletic Extra-Curriculum, 1966-1998.* They were W.T. White, the Brown and White's star halfback, and C.F. Carman, their talented young tackle.

Both faculties dropped their eligibility challenges for every player but

Barclay. "The case against White, who played on the Demorest professional team last summer, was dismissed as insufficiently supported," *The Lafayette* reported.

The reason why Barclay was not removed from that list was that there was hard evidence linking him to the Chambersburg Maroons.

A grand total of $89.70, or about the equivalent of $2,500 dollars in today's money, was his salary for playing with the Chambersburg Maroons.

According to Courtney Michele-Smith in *A Delicate Balance*, "Barclay explained that he signed a contract to play baseball for the Chambersburg club for salary and that he received the advance payment before Lehigh and Lafayette established their eligibility agreement. When March learned about his contract, [he] informed him that the contract made him ineligible under the 1896 guidelines. Barclay then claimed that he asked the Chambersburg club for his release and tried to return his advance payment; the Chambersburg club refused and threatened him with a lawsuit for breach of contract."

Lafayette was satisfied that Barclay, a student in good standing and additionally a student of regular undergraduate age, not even 21 years old, was not a professional baseball player. But Lehigh saw Barclay as someone who was paid to play sports, and thus not an amateur athlete, and in violation of the clause in their agreement with Lafayette that all the competitors have not played sports "for a financial consideration."

The revelation caused a firestorm in the local and national press.

An oft-repeated article from *The Illustrated American* was immensely damaging to Lafayette's national perception at the time. "As for Lafayette, her team deserves the highest credit, or at least it would if it were not for the unfortunate taint of professionalism," writer Chas E. Patterson said. "Barclay, one of her mainstays, is an out-an-out professional baseball player, and is one of those always suspicious students whose name in the catalogue is accompanied by some such apologetic explanation as 'Not a candidate for a degree; permitted to recite.'"

Lehigh's *Brown and White* gleefully added fuel to the fire under a November 12th headline reading "Lafayette Purity." There they recounted the circumstances as to how Fieldling Yost returned to West Virginia after leaving Easton, as told by the *Pittsburg Dispatch*. "My ankle was injured in the Pennsylvania game, and the physicians said I was crippled for the season," Yost reportedly stated. "On returning to my home in Fairmont, West Virginia to vote, I found my ankle sound enough to permit play, and at once returned to the West Virginia Varsity."

Conversely, *The Lafayette* claimed that Lehigh was simply trying to get out of the games because Barclay, who was a huge factor in Lafayette's sweep of the Lehigh series the year before, made them seem like a team that the Brown and White could not beat. "Information was received after the

Pennsylvania game that Lehigh would endeavor to avoid a game with Lafayette this year," they opined.

The cancelling of the 1896 games left a sore spot with both teams for decades afterwards, with March going as far as mounting a defense of Barclay and his actions in his book *Athletics at Lafayette College*.

In March's mind, Barclay played "summer baseball," when Lafayette was not in session, to help Barclay make enough money to attend school. To him that did not mean he was a "professional," it was the equivalent of getting a summer job. In every other aspect of his life, he was a real student who attended Lafayette for four years who never was paid to play football.

But to Lehigh, amateurism meant not receiving pay for any sport, not least baseball. Professional baseball labored in the 1890s under the perception that it was a dirty enterprise rife with game-fixing and gambling. Some clubs were closely tied to organized crime; some players were even murdered. Barclay's association with baseball for pay, summer or not, violated their definition of amateur athlete.

Richard Harding Davis, left, Caspar Whitney, 2nd from right

Unable to come to an amicable resolution of the issue, both Lehigh and Lafayette wrote the pre-eminent sports writer of his time, Caspar Whitney of *Harper's Weekly*, looking for an answer after the 1896 season had concluded.

"In my judgment," the friend of Richard Harding Davis wrote, "Lehigh was fully justified in protesting Barclay and of subsequently cancelling the games with Lafayette when the latter insisted on playing him. If Barclay is the victim of circumstances, it is unfortunate, but all the testimony submitted and disputed... points to an unwavering conclusion that Lehigh's claim of his having received money over and above the legitimate expenses of an amateur is entirely justifiable and tenable."

That it would take a third-party moderator to solve both schools' differences shows how intense the Rivalry had become.

Lehigh opposed playing Lafayette that year because, in their minds, they were no longer similar institutions. To them, Lafayette had compromised academic standards by hiring professionals.

But Lafayette saw things differently. Unlike many of the football players of his day, Barclay was a true undergraduate, who went to class and graduated from Lafayette after four years. To them, they felt Lehigh was jealous that they didn't have anyone of his caliber.

This 1896 battle over eligibility was, and is, the only year since the beginning of the Rivalry that Lehigh and Lafayette did not meet each other on the gridiron. But the sore feelings about the incident, and the ill perception of each others' programs, would continue for decades.

In the end, Lafayette was considered one of the best teams of the year 1896. The only team with a case against them was Princeton, who tied Lafayette in the beginning of the year. Both had strong wins against the best teams in the East, and they would retroactively be given a mythical national championship.

To Lafayette fans of that early era, though, the 1896 team was the finest that the Maroon and White had ever suited up for the school.

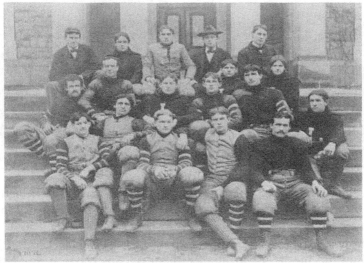

Lafayette's 1896 Football Team

10. SMOKERS

The first organized cheering during the Rivalry games appeared to come spontaneously from Lafayette and Lehigh students.

By the 1890s and the advent of professional coaches, however, faculty and coaches got more involved in cultivating spirit in their teams.

Lafayette's legendary coach Parke H. Davis, contributing to *Athletics at Lafayette College*, made no bones about his efforts to create "an intense football spirit" at Lafayette. It was one of his priorities when he was hired.

"We instituted college mass-meetings," he said. "We composed songs. At that time there were none. We invented new cheers. We bragged and blustered, orated and printed glowingly about our prospects. We worked the college and the town systematically up to a football frenzy."

Francis March considered Davis to be the person who invented the idea of "smokers."

"Smokers" were athletic pep rallies which took place on the campus to celebrate a wide variety of events, as was the custom on college campuses at the time. During these extravaganzas, the students got souvenir pipes from the smoker, as well as complimentary tobacco products.

Smokers took all colleges by storm in the 1910s, but for Lehigh and Lafayette, the history of these types of "mass-meetings" goes back further.

Before the big games versus Lehigh, the Lafayette students, organized by Davis, would meet on the grounds of their college to pass out pamphlets with the words to the latest cheers in order to rehearse them for the following day's game.

By 1897, Lehigh would be doing the same.

Eventually these would evolve into "smokers."

At Lafayette, these involved specialized songs, written by coaches and athletics representatives which were then were rehearsed and unleashed at football games.

It would be 1898 when Lafayette instituted a smoker for the expressed purpose of raising spirit for the games against Lehigh.

"A college smoker was held on Friday evening, November 4, in old Frank. Hall, under the auspices of the Dramatic Association," *The Lafayette* reported. "The original purpose of holding the trials for nomination to the Dramatic Association having been abandoned, the smoker was devoted to raising enthusiasm for the Lehigh game. This object was very effectually accomplished."

LAST AND PEPPIEST
SMOKER
TONIGHT AT 7.30

It is your duty to be there!

Ad for a Lehigh "Smoker" from the Brown and White

Lafayette would beat the Brown and White 11-5 that season, so naturally the alumni of Lehigh would organize a smoker themselves for the following season with the specific purpose of building spirit for beating Lafayette. (It did not work.)

"The recent college smoker was by no means devoid of good results," *The Lafayette* said after their successful football win. "But to speak in plain language, let us have more. The large majority of men in college are unfamiliar with most of our songs, and since we have no printed collection at the present time, another college smoker would be the means of making them known. To be unacquainted with our songs seems somewhat of a degenerate spirit, and in no better way can a democratic spirit be cultivated than by holding such college assemblies."

At Lehigh, "smokers" took place in the gymnasium, but did not have anything to do with football at first. They offered free tobacco and pipes for all present, and instead involved wrestling and boxing matches only.

As smokers evolved at both schools, basketball games were also played versus the sophomores and juniors, helping to develop both the Brown and White's and Maroon and White's first basketball teams.

The idea of "smoker" pep rallies as linked to the Rivalry seem to have morphed over time.

The first documented Lehigh "smoker" of this sort predated Lafayette's football-specific ones.

"The evening's entertainment began at a quarter after eight, when Yorks, '98, and Moritz, '98, appeared upon the floor for a sparring contest," *The Brown and White* reported in the spring of 1895. "This event was rather amusing, as neither of the contestants weighed over ninety pounds."

By 1902, smokers involving football and other sports were becoming the norm.

Tobacco companies were frequent advertisers in *The Brown and White*, and also had a cozy relationship with college football in general. Always looking to associate their products with sports, they included inserts of popular colleges and their theme songs in their products as "silks."

"The last college smoker was more of the nature of a business meeting," *The Brown and White* reported that year. "No such element will enter into the proceedings this time. It will be all fun and no work."

Part of the spirit-raising involved singing songs where each individual class would be given a different part to sing. Only during the smoker did the classes know how all the pieces would fit together for the Lafayette game.

"The committee has arranged a programme [sic] for this event that will surpass their efforts on previous occasions of this kind," *The Brown and White* also said. "A basket ball [sic] game will be played between two

Lehigh Silk on a Tobacco Card, 1900s

picked teams, from the sophomore and freshman classes. Boxing and wrestling will afford a part of the entertainment. Also club swinging by Brunner and Lord."

As Lehigh's football teams struggled in the late 1920s, the smokers were critical in keeping up spirit as the students enthusiasm waned in general concerning the Brown and White sports teams.

"Tommy Burke, the football captain, took charge of the [smoker]," *The Brown and White* reported in 1927. "He told just how much Lehigh smokers usually meant to the students, what their purpose was, and what future smokers and pep meetings were going to be held. He then introduced Bill Billmeyer, president of the senior class, who made a brief speech dwelling on the facts that there is not enough pep in the student body, and that the cheer leaders are not showing as much co-ordination as they should at games."

Freshman team head coach (and future head football coach) Austin Tate did not mince words, either. "The keynote to Lehigh sports should be optimism," he said during one smoker. "There is too cynical an atmosphere among the students; wisecracking individuals go around doing anything but trying to support the teams," - a statement that did not inspire much "pep" from the students in attendance.

Smokers served as a way to unite the students and alumni and to educate them as to the role of athletics at the school and among the alumni. They were also used to celebrate the careers of some of the more important pioneers of the athletic department.

One smoker in particular meant a great deal to one of Lehigh's faculty, Howard R. "Bosey" Reiter.

Reiter was a football pioneer who, as an undergraduate, was a star halfback at Princeton.

In 1910 he coached Lehigh's football team, and in 1911 accepted President Henry Drinker's proposal to become the first professor of physical education on the campus. In this capacity, he is considered to be Lehigh's first athletic director.

Shortly after Bosey arrived, he would hire his successor as football coach in 1921, "Tom" Keady from Dartmouth, who, over his eight year coaching career at Lehigh, would guide the Brown and White to national relevance by being Lafayette's equal. Every season in

Howard R. "Bosey" Reiter

Keady's coaching tenure, Lehigh boasted a winning record.

Wrestling became a varsity sport at Lehigh during Reiter's time, and he also hired wrestling's first full-time head coach, Billy Sheridan. Sheridan would remain at Lehigh for 42 years, guiding the wrestling team to become a national power. Sheridan's many EIWA championships and hosting of the NCAA wrestling championships helped define Lehigh athletics for several generations.

Bosey would play a large part in developing Lehigh's lacrosse program, too. He hired Lehigh's first-ever full time head coach, and during his time they would win five national championships.

He was also critical in building up spirit in the Rivalry among both the undergraduates and alumni by setting up the programs for these smokers, lining up football coaches and former stars like Walter Okeson and many more. He was a frequent speechmaker in these spirit-building meetings, and also got Sheridan and the nascent wrestling program involved. Sheridan featured prominently in the smokers of Bosey's time, even early in his career when he took to the mat himself.

Bosey would work tirelessly not only with the students and alumni, but also with the members of the Bethlehem community as well.

He set up the first "Lehigh Booster Club," consisting of both children and adults, and helped start a program to involve young underprivileged kids in the neighborhood called the "Sand Hogs Brigade." Rather than have the kids sneak into the games (by burrowing under the fences, hence their name), he gave them a set of rules to follow (for example, keeping their hands washed and clean), and giving them their own section in Taylor Stadium.

His actions ensured that Lehigh would have a large influence in Bethlehem in terms of attracting future students, including athletes.

He was so beloved that, at one smoker in 1923, Bosey was presented with a Ford car - a gift from his grateful students, who saw him ride his old beat-up bicycle to work every day and wanted to surprise him.

"He said, 'It wasn't the gift, but when, and how I got it,'" his yearbook tribute in the Lehigh Epitome of 1923 read. "...just before the Lafayette game, after a hard season. That Ford is priceless and means more than any other car in the world to him. The signatures of most of the men in college, following the testimonial that went with them is a tribute which time cannot erase."

Ultimately, smokers would go from being general pep rallies and celebrations, organized whenever the mood hit, to becoming very closely associated with the Rivalry - the union of the football season and the wrestling season.

11. PARKE DAVIS ERA ENDS GLORIOUSLY IN THE SLUSH

No smoker would make it any easier to be a fan of the Maroon and White in 1898.

It was the year the trial went forward in Easton of a former Lafayette professor who attempted to burn down Pardee Hall. His acts of vandalism and terrorism earned him six years in jail.

It was the summer when the main fighting in the Spanish-American War occurred. General Charles Augustus Wilkoff, a Lafayette alumnus and resident of Easton, was killed leading his men while preparing for an attack on San Juan Hill. (It was the scene of the battle which would make Theodore Roosevelt a household name, and Richard Harding Davis a legendary war correspondent.)

Unrest also came from the students, too. The clamor for indoor plumbing grew, with students considering it deplorable that their residential hall toilets were still outside. "It seems almost like an exaggerated piece of irony," an editorial from *The Lafayette* said, "that the Seniors should be offered courses in sanitary engineering. True sanitation, like charity, should begin at home."

If anyone attending Lafayette was hoping to get an inkling of inspiration from their football team to distract them from their situation, they would be disappointed – at least at the beginning of the season.

As Wilkoff was laid to rest on a rainy day in October, and the plans for yet another renovation of Pardee Hall were drawn up, Lafayette had to find a way to beat Lehigh on Thanksgiving Day.

Gone were many of the legendary football players on those championship teams. Charles "Babe" Reinhart and George "Rose" Barclay were lost to graduation. Only Ed Bray, the fullback, punter and kicker, remained.

The football exploits of the Maroon and White, on the other hand, were no longer being written up in the biggest papers of the time: *The New York Times*, *Harper's Weekly*, or *This Sporting Life*.

Pardee Hall on Fire, 1898

Though the players did not know it, their legendary head coach, Parke H. Davis, was also getting ready to retire at the end of the season to set up his law practice, according to *Athletics at Lafayette College*.

Davis, who would become one of the important chroniclers of early football after his retirement, knew his 1898 squad needed to be rebuilt from scratch after Reinhart and Barclay graduated.

After losing to Dickinson at home 12-6, prospects in Easton seemed to be as gloomy as the goings-on at the campus, and the negative momentum carried over to the 28th meeting between Lehigh and Lafayette.

Though Lehigh did not have a great team that season either, they had plenty to be able to "withstand the rushes of the Maroon and White" in their first meeting with Lafayette in 1898, according to *The Brown and White*. They dominated Lafayette in Bethlehem 22-0 for their first victory of their last five attempts.

"The whole Lehigh team moved as a machine," the student paper crooned, "while the visitors, especially after the removal of Bray, seemed a trifle disorganized. At no time after the first few moments of play was Lafayette at all dangerous."

Down and out, it seemed like a winter of discontent was about to descend on the Maroon and White.

Until Thanksgiving, that is.

Whether spurred on by his final game at Lafayette or simply because he wanted to reverse the tide of losing to Lehigh, Davis pulled out all the coaching stops to prepare his team for the game.

He brought in three other head football coaches that were in-between jobs to help prepare and motivate his players: George Brooke (a star fullback at Penn), Louis Vail, and Dr. Silvanus Blanchard Newton.

He would also be helped by something unexpected on the Lafayette Athletic Grounds.

"The game was played in several inches of slush," *The Brown and White* said, "and the heavy snow storm almost hid the players from the view of those in the grandstand."

"Ulsters, heavy coats, mackintoshes, gum boots, umbrellas, and even horse blankets were called into service," *The Lafayette* reported, "yet even these failed to give sufficient protection against the driving rain and snow."

As officials cleared the snow in order to reveal the boundary lines, the captains, Bray for Lafayette and Charles Chamberlain of Lehigh, headed to midfield for the coin toss. Lehigh won the toss, and Chamberlain elected to receive. Bray picked the wind direction.

With the wind in their faces in the first half, Bray did not punt the ball for Lafayette. Instead, a more inexperienced player would kick into the wind and snow. His kicks were deeply affected by the weather.

"Carter punted straight up in the air, going out of bounds on Lafayette's 10 yard line," is how *The Brown And White* described a first-half punt by Lafayette.

Eventually, that loss of field position would lead to Lehigh's only score.

"By a pretty run through the whole team," the student account continued, "aided by fine interference, he succeeded in placing the ball behind the goal posts."

Lehigh was only up 5-0 at halftime (based on the scoring system of the time), but fresh off the bench in the second half with the gale at his back, Bray changed the entire game for the Maroon and White with his punting game.

Due to the ineffectiveness of their offense – they had only earned three first downs all game - Davis elected to punt it with Bray on first down every time, with the wind at their backs.

As a result, the Maroon and White would end up gaining field position each time Bray would kick. Eventually, Lehigh's punt returner would fumble the ball attempting to field one of them.

That turnover would be the key to the game.

Lafayette would recover the ball and quickly capitalize with a touchdown and conversion to go ahead 6-5.

Once Lafayette had the lead, it would be Lehigh trying to drive into the snowstorm to win the game. They would not succeed.

Fittingly, the deciding field goal would be kicked by Bray, using a brand-new method of converting kicks.

It was one of the coaches Davis brought in, Dr. S.B. Newton, who would invent the "placement kick," an innovation that revolutionized the game of football. It increased a team's chance of scoring on a kicking play and also changed the risky nature of scoring from the foot.

This innovation was to include a "holder" holding the ball in place while the kicker would boot it through the uprights.

Placement Kicker Ed Bray

"Captain Best, the holder, and Bray, the kicker, scraped away the four inches of slush and snow so the ball could be placed on the ground for an attempt," *Legends of Lehigh - Lafayette* said. "The visibility [on the 35 yard field goal] was so poor that the crowd at first was silent, not knowing exactly what had happened. Several minutes later, the word spread that the kick was good, and the crowd exploded for the amazing feat (or foot) of Ed Bray."

Lafayette would win that game 11 to 5, and send the Maroon and White victorious to end the season, or in a "blaze of glory," as Davis would later put it.

"Notwithstanding the cold and dampness, the snow and sleet, fully 800 people turned out to see Lafayette defeat Lehigh on Thursday, thus wiping out the disgrace of November 5th, by ending a season of successive defeats with one grand, glorious victory," *The Lafayette* said.

It would also usher in the next great Rivalry head coach.

12. S.B. NEWTON'S FLYING MEAT AXE

Lafayette didn't have to wait long to stay removed from the national stage after beating Lehigh, due to one of the four coaches that Davis brought in to help the Maroon and White beat Lehigh in 1898.

Dr. Sylvanus B. Newton, a former Penn football player, Phi Beta Kappa member and football strategist, "made such an impression upon those in charge at Lafayette that he was invited to be their coach the following fall," Francis March wrote in *Athletics at Lafayette College*.

Sylvanus, or Samuel, as he was also known, accepted, and didn't waste much time in returning Lafayette to the national limelight.

"He talked football during the day, and dreamed football at night," March fondly remembered, also calling him "the cleverest head football coach that Lafayette has ever had."

He did not only bring the innovation of the placement kick with him to Lafayette.

He also brought with him an important mass momentum play that had briefly lofted Penn to the top of the football world: the "guards back" formation.

An old *Boston Herald* article details the brutal, mass momentum formation.

"It started with only the necessary five men in the line--the centre, guards, and tackles," it said. "At a given signal, the right guard ran back from the line and took up a position in the backfield, while the right halfback jumped in and filled his position temporarily, thereby fulfilling the provision of the rules that five men must be in the scrimmage at the start of a play."

Then the ball would be snapped to the quarterback.

"The right guard dashes forward," the article continued, "receives the ball from the quarterback as he passes him, and plunges into the opening at the right of centre with his head down for all he is worth. Meanwhile the right end, fullback, left halfback, left end and quarterback fall in behind him and push. Thus a wedge of six men is hurled at the opposing line like a flying meat axe. No human frame could withstand the momentum of this onslaught. It can be readily seen that under the old rule of five yards in three downs no ordinary defense methods could keep a team with this attack from marching down the field for touchdowns almost at will."

Dr. S. B. Newton

With Dr. Newton guiding the "team work, not star work," as he was fond of saying, the Maroon and White quickly remained in the national picture.

The Maroon and White coasted to a 12-1 season in 1899, their only blemish a 12-0 loss to Princeton. But their "guards back" formation allowed them to plow through most of the teams on their schedule - including their two most important games of the year.

"The story of Lehigh's defeat may be told in these few words; guards back did it all and the inability of our line to stand the continuous plunges of 'guards left' and 'guards right' explains the result," *The Brown and White* reported after the first game, a 17-0 shutout.

"In defeating Lehigh on Saturday last, Lafayette achieved her sixth consecutive victory over the Brown and White," *The Lafayette* reported after the 35-0 drubbing in the second game. "Lehigh was so completely snowed under, that there is no room for doubt as to the eminent superiority of Captain Bray's team."

Newton guided Lafayette to back-to-back winning seasons in 1900 and 1901, not only beating Lehigh soundly, but shutting them out each time, as the Brown and White had no answer to "guards back" and the stellar play of the Maroon backs.

Harry Trout, Lafayette's guard that played "back," helped pave the way for fullback David Cure and halfback James "Senator" Platt for repeated big gains.

"Every man on the team played brilliantly," *The Lafayette* reported after a 41-0 shellacking of Lehigh to close the 1901 season. "Gains of five, ten, and twenty yards were too numerous to mention, but Platt's runs of forty-five and fifty yards, respectively, and Raub's of forty and thirty-five yards were pretty pieces of work."

Guard Harry Trout

In 1902, though, Lehigh boosters would find the only way possible to slow down Lafayette.

They gathered up enough money to offer to double S.B. Newton's salary, an amount of money that Lafayette could not match.

At the time, there was no ruling structure to keep outside entities from hiring another team's coach, so if determined boosters wanted to pool their money together to hire him away, they could.

"This was much resented at Lafayette but Dr. Newton personally was not blamed," March wrote in *Athletics at Lafayette College*. "Some of the Lafayette athletic committee thought that Dr. Newton should have given Lafayette an opportunity to meet the Lehigh offer, but Dr. Newton knew financial conditions at Lafayette, and he knew very well that Lafayette could not then afford to pay the salary that Lehigh had offered."

The ploy by Lehigh's boosters paid off immediately.

In 1902 Newton's keen football mind guided Lehigh to a 7-2-1 record. Most importantly, he gave the Brown and White the upper hand going into their game against Lafayette, whose record was 6-0.

With "guards back" in the Lehigh's playbook, the Brown and White were able to crush much of their competition the same way they did in the days when they were allowed to institute their own mass momentum play, the old "Lehigh V."

The Brown and White beat Albright 83-0 and Villanova 71-0. Only

Princeton and Penn, with their championship-caliber players, could keep Lehigh down.

For the first time in the history of the Rivalry, in 1902, Lehigh and Lafayette elected to only play each other once in a season. The reason both schools agreed to do this, according to the book *Legends of Lehigh - Lafayette*, is that the game had grown so violent and injury-riddled that it was detrimental to both sides to play two games. Only one game was deemed practical to prevent injury.

Lehigh Football Team of 1902

The crowd of 1,400 Lehigh fans took the L.V.R.R. special to Easton quietly, according to *The Brown and White*. "In the front car was the forty-six strong, faces cut and bruised and artistically decorated with the occasional black eye. Little talking here, either."

After arriving at the station and then changing into their uniforms in the Lafayette gymnasium, the team joined the fans in marching up the hill to the college. On their way to the field, The Allentown Band sang "Everybody Takes His Hat Off to Lehigh."

"A few minutes of waiting, a few interchanges of cheers, and the teams on which the hopes and the joys of the rival colleges depended trotted quickly out on the field," *The Brown and White* said. "Clad in rusty jerseys, stained with the dirt of nine hard-fought games, the Lehigh team looked more business-like than handsome."

The two teams were evenly matched: Lafayette's bigger, better athletes, and Lehigh's well-coached team.

It would come down to an old play that Lafayette knew was coming.

"Captain Andy Farabaugh gave the signal for 'close formation,'" *The Brown and White* reported. "William Brush, left end for Lehigh, seized the ball, slid cautiously around the struggling bunch of legs and arms, and was down the field like a flash. Raub, winner of the 220 yard dash for Lafayette last year, was after him in an instant. Only thirty yards to go and Raub gaining at every step."

"At the 5 yard line," they continued, "the Maroon and White arms went out and caught the Brown and White stockings. In a moment both men had fallen and were rolling over and over from the momentum of their run. When they finally came to rest, the ball was planted two feet over the coveted goal line of Lafayette."

It would be the only scoring of the game – Lehigh's first points against Lafayette since that fateful game in 1898 - and it would be enough to win, causing the Lehigh fans to rush the field to surround their team.

"No [victory] bell sound came from the [Lafayette] belfry," *The Brown and White* said, "which had so often sounded the knell of Lehigh hopes. Nothing was heard but the funeral echoes from the field, where the sons of Lafayette were singing their Alma Mater with grief in their hearts."

Newton was proud of his team, too.

"The victory was the outcome of a season of hard and faithful work," he wrote the team in an open letter published in *The Brown and White*. "Lehigh played better ball, deserved to win, and did. To the men of the football squad and to the coaches who have so unselfishly given us their time and advice the University owes unlimited thanks and praise, and so do I."

Newton and Lehigh would celebrate two straight wins against Lafayette, but by the end of 1903 college football was changing.

Always a violent sport, record numbers of injuries were now happening on football teams across the nation, and Lehigh and Lafayette were no exception.

"Our hospital list has never contained more Varsity players," *The Brown and White* reported after a particularly lopsided loss to Princeton in 1904, which included two star players leaving with a broken leg and another with a broken collarbone. "Twenty minutes before the time for the train to leave South Bethlehem, Herman, end on the Varsity, telephoned to Dr. Newton that owing to the objections of his parents he would not be able to play for the remainder of the season."

Lehigh also saw its faculty start to get more involved in enforcing eligibility for membership on the football team.

Two players who expected to be a big part of the football team in the 1904 season flunked out and were not allowed to play.

On the other hand, Lafayette's football team, coached by Dr. Alfred E. Bull, was competing to be one of the best teams in the country.

Bull was an early Penn football star who coached at Iowa, Franklin & Marshall, and Georgetown before having Franklin March convince him to head to Lafayette.

Lafayette Head Coach Alfred Bull

His essay written to March in the history *Athletics at Lafayette College* included how he did so well against Lehigh, winning four straight games from 1904 to 1907.

"To add a little variety and get some much-needed help, an arrangement was entered into after the Penn-Lafayette game in 1904 to have an exchange of coaches between the two institutions," he said in his essay, "I spent a couple of days a week on a couple of occasions helping out at Franklin Field while on those occasions Wharton, Reynolds, and others at the Penn coaching staff took my place. This was productive of much good to both football squads."

The part that Coach Bull left out was that the "coaching exchange" happened right before the Lehigh game, giving Lafayette not only the benefit of two different paid coaching staffs working with their players, but also an opportunity to compare notes and scout the Brown and White.

The 1904 game was delayed a week when Lehigh's president, Dr. Thomas Drown, a former Lafayette chemistry professor, died suddenly after undergoing a surgical procedure at his home. The funeral of the beloved president, who saved Lehigh from ruin after a series of financial panics during his presidency, was the cause of the delay, but strategically it gave Lafayette more time to study their Rivals.

In the early days of the automobile and well before film was commonly available, scouting opponents was a rare luxury. Only a coach that could take a train to a game that wasn't too far away – and a coach with such faith in his staff that they could lead the team to a victory in his absence – could do so on rare occasions.

Lehigh was struggling with injuries and "retired players" - whether by choice or by failed academics - Lafayette had no problem enacting revenge on the Brown and White in 1904 by a 40-6 score.

"Before almost ten thousand people, Lafayette administered one of the most decisive defeats of the season to her old rival, Lehigh, on Thanksgiving Day," *The Lafayette* reported. "Forty to six tells the tale and tells it truly, Lehigh earned her score in the first half, and played Lafayette to a standstill, but her rout in the second half was so complete, that not once in the last thirty-five minutes of play was her team able to make two successive first downs, or force Lafayette to surrender the ball on downs."

Though the game was delayed a week and played on Thanksgiving Day, 10,000 people still came to Easton to watch the game. Lehigh fans came up with a new cheer based on a popular song at the time called 'Yow, Lehigh,' "which was a cross

Thomas Drown

between a screech of triumph and a howl of defeat, but probably intended for the former as it was not heard after the first half," *The Lafayette* said.

Hints of the current brutality of the game, was in evidence, too, however. "Some idea of the fierceness of the struggle may be gained from the fact that only five men out of the original line-up of each team were on the field at the call of time," *The Brown and White* noted.

In 1905, Henry S. Drinker, an 1871 Lehigh graduate and a key trustee who guided Lehigh through its dark financial times of the 1890s, was named president of the school.

At first it was unclear whether President Drinker would be the friend to football that President Drown was through the tough years, but it became obvious as time went on that he would let his faculty, not the football coaches, dictate athletics policy at Lehigh.

"A winning football team, or proficiency in other sports, cannot be classed as a valuable asset for a college," Drinker was reported saying in *The New York Times* later in his career. "It is merely an incident pleasing to undergraduates and alumni without appreciable effect on the student [enrollment]."

Further evidence of President Drinker's feelings about football came out during that critical year.

Lehigh's record in 1905 was 6-7, with their squad struggling. Part of the reason was a new policy of limited practice time after classes, implemented by the faculty over alumni wishes.

A 53-0 defeat at the hands of Lafayette, their second straight big loss to their Rivals, caused Newton to resign after the 1905 season.

But the big news in 1905 for college football happened after the season.

NYU's president, Henry S. MacCracken, saw a football player die during the course of a

Henry S. Drinker

football game. The unfortunate student was a Union College player named Harold Moore.

"Moore was injured about the middle of the game," the *Washington Post* reported, "when the contest was closest and the play fiercest. In an attempt to get through the New York center Moore went at the line head first like a catapult. This play was his last. No one saw what Moore's head struck but he dropped limply to one side of the scrimmage and the ball fell from his hands. All efforts to revive him failed. The spectators became so excited that they poured on the gridiron by the hundreds, until the police drove them back."

Moore died six hours later at Fordham Hospital.

Shortly after the student's death, MacCracken looked to convene school leaders in an effort to rein in and reform athletics in colleges. It was an effort that President Drinker, and Lehigh's faculty, eagerly joined.

MacCracken's efforts faced resistance from Harvard and Yale, who largely wished football to remain the way it was with the same people running the show. Undeterred, MacCracken held a series of conventions, attempting to either "reform football, or abolish it," according to Ronald A. Smith's *Journal of Sports History*.

Professor Charles L. Thornburg, Lehigh's representative, joined sixty-three other delegates at MacCracken's conventions. Thornburg, one of the faculty members that protested George Barclay's eligibility back in 1896, was a member of Lehigh's alumni athletic committee and attended as a fan of football who wished to revise the rules, not abolish the sport.

Henry S. MacCracken

These conventions, held as a challenge to Walter Camp's own rules committee, was a driving force to help form a set of standardized rules that would govern athletics. These included eligibility rules, playing rules to improve the safety of the game, and other technical aspects of football, such as the length of the field and the number of points for touchdowns and conversion kicks.

MacCracken led a series of meetings which helped form the IAAUS, a grouping of thirty-three schools that agreed to play by standardized eligibility rules and regulations. The IAAUS, which would ultimately become the NCAA, counted Lehigh as one of its first members.

Lafayette was not a member of this initial push to create a centralized body with uniform rules, however. President Ethelbert D. Warfield, the man who had founded the football program at Miami of Ohio, had no desire to change the game that he loved, especially when he saw it vital to maintaining enrollment at his small school.

According to the reformers, the idea of offering "scholarships" to student-athletes was starting to be considered counter to the principles of amateurism and against the integrity of an institution of higher learning.

In contrast to the opinions of the reformers, President Warfield enthusiastically endorsed scholarships at Lafayette, going as far as actually controlling the scholarship process. This allowed him to offer an education for any potential football player with need – but the level of need was determined by President Warfield.

Eventually, Lafayette would join what would become the NCAA, succumbing to the pressures of reform, along with Harvard, Princeton, and all the Eastern institutions of higher learning.

But until they did, it made for some unhappy Rivalry games for Lehigh and a good time for Lafayette supporters in an era where the game was changing rapidly.

From 1906 to 1911, Lafayette would win six of seven games against Lehigh, and in all five victories the Maroon and White would win by double-digits.

A new strategy was being tried by both sides in the Rivalry, now legal in the standardized rules: the forward pass. In 1906, coaches everywhere were trying to figure out how to best exploit the rule changes to their advantage by attempting different styles and strategies.

While most schools were learning how to execute forward passes similar to basketball players performing a chest pass, Howard R. "Bosey" Reiter, as head coach at Wesleyan, was developing the "overhead spiral pass" for his players.

The passing style he invented, where the quarterback throws the ball with his dominant arm, starting from his ear and throwing the ball in the direction of a receiver, is the type of passing that is well-known today.

The first-ever forward pass thrown in the Rivalry was performed, according to *The Brown and White*, by Lehigh. "A forward pass netted a first down for the Brown and White," the student writer wrote in his play-by-play of the game.

It's likely the first-ever pass would have been thrown by Lehigh quarterback Arthur Fulton to captain Frank Edgar Troutman. Neither Lehigh's or Lafayette's student accounts of the game say for certain that these were the two players involved in the pass.

What was clear, though, is that Lafayette did not need a forward pass to dominate Lehigh that season, easily cruising to a 33-0 victory.

Lafayette's quarterback, Edward Flad, connected with Andy Chalmers, the former captain of the Iowa football team, for the Maroon and White's first pass completion. (Iowa was coached at that time by Andy's brother, John Chalmers.)

In 1907, the first interception return for a touchdown would occur when star Lafayette running back/defensive back George McCaa returned an errant Lehigh pass to score a touchdown in a 22-5 victory.

"After a short line gain," *The Lafayette* reported, "Anderson made a high forward pass, the ball sailing into the arms of McCaa without the latter moving an inch. In an instant the fleet back was off for Lehigh's goal, and so fast did he run that he had outsprinted all opponents after he had reached Lehigh's thirty-five-yard line, where the Brown and White gave up the chase."

McCaa, one of Lafayette's great athletes, was the equal to George

George McCaa

Barclay in the eyes of many early fans who watched him. He ran the ball extremely well and intercepted passes, too, and his punting was something remarked upon by his head coach, Bob Folwell, and many others.

Lafayette's team in McCaa's senior year, 1909, would feature a squad that came extremely close to competing for a mythical national championship.

In their game against Penn, Lafayette allowed a very late touchdown to cause the contest to end in a 6-6 tie. That score would be the only points to register against the Maroon and White all season.

Oddly enough, those points were enough to prevent Lafayette from being in contention for the mythical national championship, as both Harvard and Yale were undefeated and untied going into their big rivalry game (and Yale, additionally, did not have a point scored on them all season).

With McCaa, a threat in nearly every aspect of the game in the early era of football, Lafayette bulldozed through their schedule, going 5-0-1 up until the Lehigh game.

And Lafayette, after losing surprisingly to Lehigh the prior year by an 11 to 5 margin, wasn't taking any chances in regards to overlooking their Rivalry opponents.

"The South Bethlehemites would gladly lose every other contest on their schedule if by so doing they could bring home a victory over the local team," *The Lafayette* said. "All season the whole team has been working with but this one end in view. They have had reverses, but they only smile and keep on looking toward their one object and goal—the Lafayette game."

But the third-team all-American McCaa would not play against Lehigh, since it was judged by Lafayette's faculty and head coach that he had exhausted his playing eligibility.

"Our people were getting all leery as to whether we would win, mainly because 'Mac' [McCaa] was ineligible to play in that game," Folwell recalled in *Athletics at Lafayette College*. "But the whole team had developed into a wonderful machine at that time, and just before the game I told [Franklin March] there wasn't a team in the country that could beat us."

It would be a trick play that would give Lafayette the first-ever passing touchdown of the Rivalry.

"Quarterback William Dannehower took the snap at his own 45 yard line," *Legends of Lehigh - Lafayette* said, "and pitched to Aaron Crane in the backfield, who then hurled the ball to Frank Irmshler for a touchdown."

Lafayette would shut out Lehigh in the same way they shut out nearly everyone else that season, capping off a successful year with a 21-0 victory over Lehigh even without their star player.

Additionally, March called their 1909 team a "championship" team in *Athletics at Lafayette College*. Though they were not retroactively awarded a national championship because of Yale's undefeated, unscored upon season, the 1909 squad was considered to be among the greats at Lafayette.

13. PAZZETTI SAVES THE DAY

In 1911, the Rivalry was at a point where Lafayette was a dominant force over the Brown and White.

"Last Saturday, the team saw the game between Lehigh and Franklin and Marshall," *The Lafayette* reported in the run-up to the Lehigh game, now only being played once a year. "The Brown and White was forced to play her Varsity to win and the wearers of the Maroon got a good idea of their plan of play. Not one of the locals found cause for apprehension over the contest. All are confident that Saturday will mark the season of 1911 as a success for the Eastonians."

Though *The Lafayette* very carefully guarded against overconfidence – they remembered the loss of 1908 still all too well - fans of the Maroon and White had plenty of reason to be confident.

Over the last decade, Lafayette had beaten Lehigh seven times in ten games, and was still considered one of the top teams in all of college football. In an era where Princeton, Yale, and the Carlisle Indian School all competed for the top school in the East, Lafayette was in the mix as well.

In 1911, Lehigh announced their seriousness to vault back into contention with these top teams by signing four key transfers, including a future Brown and White hall-of-fame quarterback, Pat Pazzetti, from Wesleyan.

"The Pennsylvania college [Lehigh] is pulling strongly for a record-breaking football team this year - hoping to put one on their old rival, Lafayette - and is doing all in its power to get the athletes in the institution," *The Lafayette* reported.

Lehigh entered the Lafayette game 5-3-1, but the tie, against the team that would win the paper championship in 1911, Princeton, was a great source of pride for Lehigh fans. It was played in a "sea of mud and water," according to the *Brown and White*.

Entering the 45th meeting with their Rivals, Lafayette was 6-2 and only three teams scored against them all season.

One of those teams was the Carlisle Indian School, headlined by the legendary Jim Thorpe. He played running back, defensive back, placekicker, and punter.

Lafayette and Lehigh would both face off against Thorpe's teams in 1911 and 1912, respectively.

Carlisle Indian School Football Team, 1911

"The mighty Powell and the mightier Thorpe composed a battering ram that could pierce the defense almost at will," *The Lafayette* reported in 1911 under the headline 'Lafayette Massacred by Dusky Carlisle Warriors.' "Time after time Thorpe would take the ball and charge at the opposing barrier with herculean effort, dragging with him two or three tacklers as so many playthings; his ground-gaining was invariable."

The Lafayette was impressed by Carlisle as a team, too.

"As the Indians trotted from the field house the giant stature of their players first dawned upon those who had seen them only through the newspapers," they noted. "The two teams met before a crowd of 6,000 spectators and rooters, most of them loyal friends of Lafayette but many supporters of the Indians."

The 1911 contest between Lehigh and Lafayette made for quite a game, even by Rivalry standards.

"From early morn until the time of the game," *The Brown and White* reported, "train after train brought Lehigh and Lafayette adherents by the thousands. As the time passed, the crowds increased in volume. Vast streams of humanity poured into the field at all entrances."

"It was the largest crowd that has ever assembled on Lehigh Field," *The Lafayette* added, noting that 10,000 fans attended to watch the struggle. "The cheering sections swayed and rocked as fortune favored one side or the other."

Lafayette brought a school band to perform, while Lehigh's cheering section included The Bethlehem Steel Band, a world-class outfit sponsored by the president of the company, Charles M. Schwab. At halftime, they "marched around the field and formed an "L" in the center of the gridiron," *The Brown and White* reported.

On the field, though, Lafayette's squad was too much for the Brown and White in an 11-0 win. "That aurora borealis of enthusiasm which sprung up overnight [for Lehigh] vanished in ninety-five minutes," *The Lafayette* reported. "All this constituted the pride in which fell to defeat on Lehigh Field last Saturday afternoon. Lehigh, that time honored rival of Lafayette, to-day mourns over the remains of colors trampled in the mud and marred beyond recognition by eleven Maroon and White warriors."

Lehigh's effort, led on the field by their quarterback, Pat Pazzetti, was mentioned by both papers. "The little quarter-back was ever on the alert. His punts were always for good distance and he usually ran back Kelly's punts for 20 yards or more."

1912 represented big changes when it came to the rules of college football. Touchdowns were now six points instead of five, and it took four downs to gain 10 yards instead of three.

Due to the increased use of the forward pass, playing fields were shortened from 110 yards to 100 yards, and end zone areas were designated. This was a key element in altering the game to allow for the development of these new innovations. "The purpose of this is to provide amply[sic] space for execution of the forward pass, and scoring on a pass made across the goal-line into this zone is permitted," *The Brown and White* said.

With the new rules and Pazzetti at the helm, Jim Thorpe's Carlisle Indians would have their chance to compete against the Brown and White.

"The Indians won the toss," *The Brown and White* reported under the headline 'Lehigh's Forward Passes Baffle Redskins', "and Thorpe kicked off to Pat Pazzetti, promptly at 3:00 o'clock.... With five yards to gain on a fourth down, Pazzetti attempted a forward pass to Vela which Thorpe intercepted, and carried eighty-five yards for a touchdown. Thorpe kicked the goal. Time, 3:04 P.M."

Lehigh would watch helplessly as Thorpe would score three touchdowns, and Carlisle's other halfback, Alex Arcasa, would add a couple more.

The year of Lehigh's game, Carlisle would end up being a national championship team. In their games against the teams from the Lehigh Valley, *The Brown and White* and *The Lafayette* both omitted the contributions of their hall-of-fame head coach, Charles "Pop" Warner, their huge guard Stan Powell, and a host of other legendary players from those teams.

By the end of the 1912 season, Lehigh seemed like they were going to be a formidable opponent for their Rivals, entering the big game with a 7-2 record.

"At last Lafayette approaches the real climax of her football season," noted *The Lafayette* on November 22nd. "The football world always watches this contest with the closest interest for it is the greatest of the annual struggles between small college teams. To the ardent supporters of these two colleges, even the Yale-Harvard game is but a minor incident in comparison to the deciding of this championship. No matter how many games Lehigh may lose during the season, she always tackles Lafayette with a sturdy confidence and hope of victory. No matter how many great games Lafayette wins in the season she always enters this struggle ready to fight,

World's Greatest Athlete

Captain
Carlisle Indian Football Team
Picture of Jim Thorpe in The Brown and White

knowing that upon the outcome depends the real success or failure of the season and knowing that her opponents will be worthy of every possible effort."

After an era of near-complete dominance by Lafayette in the Rivalry, the roles of the Brown and White and the Maroon and White were suddenly reversed in 1912, and the student writer at *The Lafayette* knew it.

"Sweeping victories for the past three years have caused Lafayette to assume a rather superior feeling toward Lehigh," the reporter said. "Not so this year. Lehigh has the best team that has represented that institution in the past ten years."

Going into the Lafayette game, it was Lehigh's defense that really stood out, including shutout wins over Navy, 14-0, and Swarthmore, 3-0, two very strong teams of the time.

"Defeat was bitter for the Middies, as it was the first one their team had suffered for three seasons, and many of them had never seen their eleven beaten," *The Brown and White* reported. "Nearly all of the plays were started from a formation of the backs similar to the old kick formation, and in nearly every case the man with the ball had little or no help. The skill displayed by Captain Pazzetti in leading the team, and his remarkable gains with the ball were features of the game."

"Lehigh broke Swarthmore's winning streak last Saturday afternoon on Whittier Field at Swarthmore in one of the most exciting games ever seen there, by administering a 3 to 0 defeat to the Garnet team," *The Brown and White* said. "Undoubtedly the most conspicuous player in the game was Captain Pazzetti, who, in the last period of play kicked the field goal that brought victory to the Brown and White eleven."

Pat Pazzetti Leading the Lehigh Offense, 1912

While the paper's praise mostly was heaped on Pazzetti, the coaching and use of "interference" was pioneered by Tom Keady. Keady coached the Brown and White for eight seasons before embarking on a hall-of-fame thirty-year head coaching career that would land him at Vermont, Case Western, UMass, and Dartmouth. It was in 1912 when his legend started for Lehigh.

In comparison, Lafayette entered the contest 3-5-1 and was a team racked by injury. In the game leading up to the Rivalry, a 21-7 setback to

Brown, the Maroon and White team's captain, center Howard L. Benson, did not play due to injury. Two more starters got hurt during the course of the game. "Despite the fact that Brown won, there is no word but praise for the valiant fight the team made under such overwhelming odds," *The Lafayette* reported.

Still, there was no yield from Lafayette in the run-up to the Rivalry game. "I feel it in my bones that we are going to beat Lehigh," Benson said in a statement to the student paper.

On the Lehigh side, entertainment in the run-up to the game was provided in the form of their traditional smoker.

"Following a number of songs and cheers for Lehigh and the team, the annual Freshman-Sophomore game of basket-ball was announced in which the Sophomores won out by the score of 30 to 15," *The Brown and White* reported. "Following a vaudeville act, a wrestling exhibition and a rousing speech by Coach Keady, the attendants then went on their annual parade through 'the Bethlehems', where they serenaded the girls of Moravian."

The L.V.R.R. Student Special train from the Lehigh Valley station took the Lehigh faithful to the game, a special 1:20 train that cost 50 cents to ride, round trip.

The Lehigh students would see a very fierce battle between the two bitter rivals, with the Brown and White, this time, coming out on top, 10-0 in front of a crowd of over 12,000 or 15,000 fans, depending on which account you read.

"For the first time since the 11 to 5 Lehigh victory in 1908, the Brown and White eleven gave Lafayette a defeat last Saturday afternoon on March Field, Easton before a record crowd," *The Brown and White* said. "Despite the fact that the Lehigh team was outweighed by far, they entered into the game from the start with the determination to fight to the end, and which was backed up by the perfect cheering of the entire college seated in the east stands."

"In one of the greatest gridiron battles of the East, the Maroon and White of Lafayette was forced to bow to the Brown and White of Lehigh last Saturday," *The Lafayette* reported. "The goal of attainment has been reached. After three years of defeat, Lehigh has succeeded in defeating her old rival, and in crossing the Maroon and White goal line the first time since 1908."

"Lehigh came to Easton fully confident of victory, realizing that the opportunity of opportunities was at hand," the paper continued, not-so-subtly implying that, perhaps, the Brown and White transferred their way to greatness. "Well fortified with one of the strongest elevens in the history of the institution, built around Hoban, the old Dartmouth halfback, Sawtelle from Georgetown, Pazzetti, the old Wesleyan quarterback, McCaffrey from the same institution, and Keady, a Texas College man, Lehigh presented an aggregation of players well worth the best of opposition."

Following a ticket dispute, which was solved when Lafayette finally made 400 more tickets available to Lehigh on the day before the game, the stands were packed. In attendance was Lafayette College's band, and many "feminine partisans," according to *The Lafayette*. "Every seat was occupied and thousands were standing. Massed on the west side of the field was the Maroon and White legion, and on the east side the Brown and White adherents were gathered."

"In the third quarter, when Captain Pazzetti sent the ball rocketing between the uprights for a field goal, all the pent-up energy of four years burst forth and pandemonium reigned in the Lehigh stands," *The Lafayette* reported. Pazzetti's pass to Sawtelle (the first touchdown pass ever recorded by Lehigh in the Rivalry) resulted in an ovation by the Lehigh fans, according to *The Brown and White*. "It was not until that

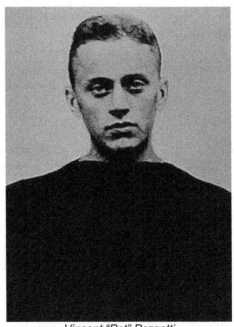

Vincent "Pat" Pazzetti

pass that the confidence of victory by the Maroon and White was shaken," *The Lafayette* said.

"Lafayette has been so accustomed to victory over Lehigh that it was rather hard to be entirely generous and be happy even in defeat," *The Lafayette* reported.

"After four years of climbing, Lehigh has won," a gushing *Brown and White* reported. "After years of working against odds, and heavy ones, Lehigh's loyal sons have succeeded in putting onto the field a team which has proven itself the conqueror of Lafayette in one of the most desperately fought games that was ever played between the old rivals. When Pazzetti's magnificent place-kick went spinning between the Lafayette goal-posts, the hardships of past endeavors were forgotten, uphill climbing was but a memory. We had beaten Lafayette - and joy knew no bounds."

14. THE RIVALRY THROUGH THE GREAT WAR

Initially, it did not seem conceivable that war in Europe would affect the daily lives of American boys and men playing college football in Pennsylvania.

Before World War I broke out, or the Great War as it was then called, President Woodrow Wilson pursued a strict policy of neutrality in regards to the trench battles in Belgium and France, echoing popular opinion.

But when a world war became inevitable, it affected the campuses of Lafayette and Lehigh deeply in the seasons of 1917 and 1918.

Through the seriousness of war, the Rivalry continued where other college football seasons were halted, complete with much of the same pageantry.

In tough times, the Rivalry provided a much-needed escape.

Woodrow Wilson started his rise to the Presidency through academia, first at Bryn Mawr College and then at Wesleyan College.

Though he never competed on the gridiron, he was an avid football fan.

After a particularly poor start to the 1889 football season at Wesleyan, the young history teacher reportedly "injected himself into the [football] situation as faculty adviser." This story made the rounds through several newspapers in the 1910s.

More provable was his dedication to forming football strategy, attending practices, and making trips to some out-of-town games in the horse and

141

buggy era.

Woodrow Wilson and a graduate assistant even coined a slogan for the college, according to a biography of him by Edwin A. Weinstein: "The College First, The Fraternity Afterward."

Wesleyan's 1889 football season came to a head with a critical game against Lehigh, the Brown and White team with legendary halfback Paul Dashiell. Lehigh was legitimately considered to be one of the top teams in the nation that year.

As legend had it, down 11-0 to the Brown and White on a rainy afternoon in Springfield, Massachusetts, Wilson, clad in a rubber raincoat and boots, led Wesleyan's cheering section in a group of rousing cheers, his umbrella tapping to the beat.

The players, allegedly inspired by the display from Wilson, and feeling they needed the result to stay relevant in the world of college football, rallied late to secure an 11-11 tie.

Oliver Schmidt Illustration of "Woodrow Wilson, Football Coach," 1912

Few that day might have thought that the progressive Wilson would become the Commander in Chief after that exhibition on the football field. But that is what happened, with his meteoric rise through academia.

At Princeton, he would continue to be an advocate for their football team. In *The Philadelphia's Public Ledger*, Wilson extolled the virtues of the game, saying it "develops more moral qualities than any other game of athletics…This game produces…qualities not common to all athletics, that of co-operation, or action with others, and self-subordination. These are things to be encouraged, and they unquestionably come from the game of football."

As president of Princeton, Wilson instituted some important reforms that were a springboard to his public life, and ultimately, the presidency of the United States in 1913.

By 1917, the pacifist President Wilson, facing increased German U-boat provocation in the Atlantic Ocean, could not hold off American involvement in the Great War any longer.

Army Chief of Staff Peyton C. March

One of Wilson's acts as president was to promote a former Lafayette football player to Brigadier General of the Army.

Peyton C. March, the fullback on Lafayette's first team to suit up against Lehigh, had a stellar military career that saw him perform strategy in the Philippines, the Spanish-American War, and the Russo-Japanese War. He was also the brother of Francis A. March, author of *Athletics at Lafayette College*.

By the time of the Great War, Peyton March commanded the 1st Field Artillery Brigade, 1st Infantry Division, and the American Expeditionary Forces.

A draft was instituted among men aged 21 to 31. This affected a large number of Lehigh and Lafayette students, some of whom might have gone directly into the 1st Infantry Division.

"Probably the two upper classes are the hardest hit by the departure of many of their number to the call of the government, but the Sophomore class also has lost some of its members," *The Brown and White* reported, listing a group of undergraduates who were conscripted into the National Army, Naval Aviation, and other branches of the military.

The same occurred at Lafayette, with nearby Allentown as the site of training for the U.S. Ambulance Service Corps. Lafayette students formed a "Lafayette Ambulance Unit," Unit No. 61.

"Twenty-eight men of Lafayette, bronze of face and stalwart of form," *The Lafayette* reported, "are now awaiting their turn to break camp and join an overseas contingent. The men will probably leave soon to carry the name of Lafayette College to the country from which the immortal Lafayette himself came."

As the Ambulance Corps drivers recruited both Lehigh and Lafayette students, their love of football inspired the drivers to form their own team - and compete against their former schools.

"Pitted against a team composed of former college stars and the Three Brown Brothers of Lafayette," *The Lafayette* said, "the Maroon and White's 'brand new' team on Saturday handed to their opponent a defeat in terms of 20-0. The Ambulance Team's offensive lacked unity of interference and was powerless against the other line."

Allentown Ambulance Corps Football Team, 1917

Other military units formed teams that appeared on Lehigh and Lafayette football schedules alongside more traditional opponents like Georgetown and Rutgers.

"Lehigh's 1917 gridiron season opened Saturday on Taylor Field with a 7 to 0 victory over the Seventh Infantry team, composed entirely of men from various colleges who are now second lieutenants at the army camp at Gettysburg," *The Brown and White* reported. "Considering they [Seventh Infantry] only had three days' practice and that without a competent coach, they played a hard game."

Despite the war, thousands of fans watched these games, which likely was an effective recruiting tool for the army.

Overall, Lafayette struggled in the season of 1917, due to the disappearance of most upperclassmen to the draft.

Only two men tried out for the football team that had played on the varsity the prior season. "One was drafted before the first game," *The Lafayette* stated, "and the other dropped out after one or two contests."

Maroon and White fans feared the worst for their football team's chances after a 56-0 shellacking at the hands of Swarthmore.

"In the face of war conditions, Lafayette is playing a straight schedule with her traditional opponents, without cancellations, and without soldier athletes," *The Lafayette* noted. "It is a difficult and a heartbreaking task to build a college team entirely of new men, whether or not they are experienced in preparatory school football."

Only one outcome could salvage the Maroon and White season.

"There is one game left that Lafayette men should work hard to win," the paper continued. "There is one game left that will make all the difference in the world with the final estimate of this season. To better present conditions in that game means nothing more or less than two weeks of slavery for the football team. It means a lot of continuous, secret practices, and all the strategy in planning out this coming conflict that our resources will permit. There is a great deal that Lafayette students can do. We must remember what the Lehigh game means to us. We must stand in a body back [sic] of the team when it meets the Brown and White, and no matter whether we shall sing 'Lafayette's Men All Victorious' or the 'Alma Mater' at the conclusion of the game, let there be no man who has not done his bit."

Lehigh's problems for the 1917 season did not involve players, but the schedule.

Villanova and Fordham, both scheduled to play the Brown and White, suspended their games with Lehigh when they cancelled their football seasons. The national powers, Georgetown and Pitt, did not.

Pitt, now coached by the legendary Glenn "Pop" Warner, dominated the Brown and White 41-0, while Georgetown jumped to an early lead and made it hold up, 14-6.

Despite the setbacks, there was a lot of promise for head coach Tom Keady's Lehigh squad.

"Beaten numerically, but not in spirit, the work of the team gives the impression that it has found itself and will go through the rest of the schedule at a different pace than it did through the first of the season," *The Brown and White* said.

The lead-up to the biggest game on the schedule was the same as many of the others through the years, though with less animosity between the schools.

Lehigh reported about a smoker that had been better attended than in prior years, complete with a parade through the "Bethlehems." "Bosey"

145

Reiter and Walter Okeson delivered their usual stirring speeches.

"Whatever the result, the interest in the contest will be the same," *The Brown and White* reported. "A defeat for either team means the failure of the entire season to their college. In view of the general unsettled atmosphere which was prevalent at the beginning of the term, due to the war, the support has been good and has demonstrated that the old Lehigh spirit is as strong as ever."

"The Lehigh Smoker, which, next to the game itself, is one of the biggest events of the football season, is to be held in accordance with tradition on Friday night," *The Lafayette* reported. "Prof. March has been asked to tell about other times when the Maroon and White has sent the Brown and White "back up the river" to spend another year in

Tom Keady

hopeful preparation for the Lafayette eleven. Despite the losses earlier in the season the men of the Lafayette team are as anxious to get at Lehigh as men of other years, and they will meet the rival team with as grim a determination to win as that ever possessed by any team of former years."

Determination was not enough.

"Running, dodging and plunging their way up and down Taylor Field for touchdown after touchdown," *The Brown and White* announced triumphantly, "Coach Keady's well-prepared team trampled the Maroon and White colors of Lafayette underfoot, completely outclassing the Easton collegians in one of the most remarkable Lehigh-Lafayette games seen in a quarter of a century, and winning by the overwhelming score of 78-0."

The Brown and White scored an amazing 12 touchdowns, including four by fullback Vincent de Wysocki and four by quarterback A.S. Herrington.

"If there are any features about the game, they might be said to lie in the large number of touchdowns scored, the numerous goals from touchdowns that Lehigh missed, and the almost limitless number of substitutions made by Lafayette," *The Lafayette* lamented.

The game was played in a half-empty stadium, according to the student paper, and the formal "duel of the bands" between the Lafayette students and the Bethlehem Steel Band before the game was short.

Robert Berryman

"Yet thru the four quarters of play," *The Lafayette* continued, "a time that seemed endless to Lafayette rooters, while the Brown and White were scoring so consistently and with so little resistance, the Lafayette cheering section upheld its end in a way that will never be forgotten. The true spirit of Lafayette was evidenced during that heartbreaking contest."

Lafayette's head coach, Robert Berryman, resigned after the game, though it was not due to the lopsided score.

"In his letter of resignation to the President, accepted some days ago," *The Lafayette* said, "Berryman stated that he was leaving from purely patriotic motives. There is a general demand for engineers, throughout the country and being a graduate engineer, Berryman has accepted a good position in an aeroplane construction company. Berryman expressed his gratitude for the hearty appreciation given his work here, but said that he did not believe anything should be allowed to interfere with the service of ones Country in these trying times. Before leaving, he expressed an earnest desire to return to Lafayette next fall and to continue with the work of coaching football."

As trying as the 1917 season was, 1918 was even more serious as President Wilson lowered the conscription age to 18.

"On June 21st, Lehigh University received a telegram from Adjutant General McCain in the form sent out on that date to a number of Universities and Colleges of the country," *The Brown and White* reported, "outlining a plan for sixty days' training camps from July 18 to September 16 for selected students and faculty members to be trained as instructors to help officers assigned to carry on military instruction at the institutions."

"Camp Coppée" was created at Coppée Hall to establish the Students' Army Training Corps at Lehigh, per government order.

"Oh! You Lehigh men," the student paper continued, "old and new, think of what service you will be to your country; think how proud Lehigh will be of you, if you throw all your energy and resources into the battle of democracy. Here is your chance to make good. This is not the time for trivial things."

FOOTBALL TEAM LINED UP
1918 Lehigh Football Team

It was very unclear as to whether Lehigh would have a team for the 1918 season, due to the war and the fact that many schools suspended intercollegiate football.

The stars from last season's team, Herrington and de Wysocki, were gone, drafted into the army.

"That Lehigh will be represented by a football team this year is practically certain as Captain [A.G.] Van Atta is in favor of the continuation of football as far as military training will permit," *The Brown and White* later reported. "The management is trying hard to find a suitable opponent for the opening date but is meeting with trouble on account of the earliness in the season and unsettled conditions among other colleges."

Additionally, there was considerable doubt as to whether Lehigh would field enough students to have a team, as almost everyone who played the prior year was gone, drafted, or both. But Lehigh, led by Van Atta (who also was student council president) tried out about fifty students and managed to put together a team.

Lafayette, too, managed to suit up a team despite the uncertainty.

"At the opening of the fall semester at Lafayette, it appeared that the college would be without a team," *The Lafayette* reported. "The military authorities however, stepped in and offered to help in developing an S.A.T.C. team. When the first call was sounded, one L man of the 1917 squad, one substitute and a large number of freshmen responded. But despite many misfortunes, good material was discovered, a schedule arranged and a coach selected from among the military authorities assigned to the college for instruction purposes."

Lehigh's ambitious 1918 schedule was shortened, instead facing pick-up teams from the other military training camps, and also Rutgers, Muhlenburg, Penn State, and Lafayette. The Maroon and White featured a hybrid schedule too, like Lehigh, playing service teams and the few local schools still fielding intercollegiate teams.

Lafayette Students Marching Home to Easton after the Armistice

All through the season Lehigh's smokers were well-attended by the students, who seemed headed to the European front. The smokers served as a distraction from military training, with the one leading up to the Rivalry game being the best attended of all.

"Into every available space with the exception of a small squared area in the center of the floor were crowded the student-soldiers," *The Brown and White* reported, "and music to enliven the occasion was liberally furnished by the Bethlehem Steel Band."

The 1918 game itself, which almost was cancelled, ended in Lehigh's third straight win over Lafayette, though it was a much more evenly matched 17-0 game that was devoid of some of the bitterness the Rivalry generated in peacetime.

The subdued nature of the game can be explained by another front-page item in *The Brown and White's* same edition. "Word has been received that Lieutenant John Reading Schley, of the class of 1919, has died of wounds received in an airplane accident while serving in France."

Peyton March, the former Lafayette football player, would serve with distinction in the Great War and was promoted to acting Army Chief of Staff under Wilson. He was credited with reorganizing the existing Army structure to accommodate new technologies, including the Air Corps and Chemical Warfare Corps.

With peace came a return to normalcy – and a return to sporting pastimes.

15. TWO BLOCKED KICKS SAVE THE RIVALRY

In 1927, the Rivalry was in trouble.

"Thousands of vacant seats at Saturday's game, mostly on the south side of the field, were a silent protest to Lehigh's poor teams," *The Easton Express* wrote after another lopsided Brown and White loss to the Maroon and White. "The dear public was asked to part with $4 a ticket to see Saturday's game. Of course, the public doesn't have to go. They can stay at home. That is what many did on Saturday. But there are thousands of Alumni of both institutions who deplore the situation and are crying for relief."

The game in question was a 43-0 shellacking by Lafayette, capping off a dismal 1-7-1 season for Lehigh where the Brown and White were outscored 196-31 by their opponents.

For Lehigh, losing to Lafayette had become routine. It was their eighth straight loss to their rivals. The Brown and White had last scored a touchdown against Lafayette in 1921. Three entire classes had gone without scoring a touchdown against them, let alone come close to victory.

In the span of two years, though, Lehigh would break Lafayette's spell, first by scoring their first touchdown against the Maroon and White in nearly a decade, and then by beating them in one of the closest games in Rivalry history.

Only a decade earlier, Lehigh athletics had been in a golden era, winning championships in lacrosse and wrestling, while also beating their bitter rival in football six times in a seven year stretch.

But it was a faculty decision that caused Lehigh's athletics to take a turn

151

in the other direction.

With the inauguration of President Charles Russ Richards in 1922, a few years after a tentative peace at home after the Great War, Lehigh quietly started to de-emphasize intercollegiate athletics.

In the September 26th, 1922 edition of *The Brown and White*, alongside several pages describing Lehigh's "foot-ball" prospects, was Mr. Richards' inaugural speech to Lehigh's undergraduates.

"I have often heard it asserted that a student who did indifferent work in the classroom, but who was recognized as a leader among his fellow students," Richards said, "was more likely to be successful than the student who has been characterized as a grind. While I recognize the importance of college activities and their value in training young men for leadership, I do not believe that the assumption... is generally a correct one... I urge you to regard them as incidental to rather than the chief object of your college life."

While football was not cited specifically in his speech, the mention of

Charles R. Richards

"leaders among their fellow students" was a clear shot at the football team.

Additionally, on the football schedule in place of teams like Penn State and West Virginia, opponents deemed more similar in terms of academic requirements started to show up instead, including Colgate, Bucknell, and Brown.

Lehigh students also seemed to overwhelmingly agree with Professor Richards, going as far as facing off against alumni who "take athletics too seriously, and attach too much importance to victories," Lehigh's treasurer, former football player Walter Okeson, reported in the *Lehigh Alumni Bulletin*. "Too much system, said they, tends to eliminate real sport and promote the professional spirit. Alumni demanded impossible schedules and wanted our teams to play Harvard, Yale, Princeton, Pennsylvania, Cornell, and Penn State. They fail to realize that undergraduates come to Lehigh to be educated and that sport is a secondary matter."

John B. "Jock" Sutherland

This sentiment came at a time when Lafayette was a potent force nationally in college football.

In 1921, Lafayette had an extraordinary team, which finished the season undefeated and was unquestionably the best team in the East according to the sportswriters of the time.

Coached by Dr. John B. "Jock" Sutherland, the Maroon and White's best win of the season came against Pitt, coached by Glenn "Pop" Warner in a hard-fought 6-0 win of the assistant over his former mentor.

"The big Maroon Team of Lafayette College last Saturday turned back the Pitt Panther by a 6 to 0 score and as a result becomes a strong contender for the Intercollegiate Football Championship of the East," *The Lafayette* said. "Seizing the proper moment, [Boots] Brunner pulled the unexpected on Pitt and, on a triple pass ran almost unmolested for twelve yards and a touchdown."

L.A. "Boots" Brunner, Lafayette's star halfback as named in *The Lafayette*, had been around.

Called "Bots" by *The New York Times*, (perhaps a typo), he started his collegiate career with Lehigh in 1916 before transferring to Yale and then Penn before heading back to the Lehigh Valley as a starter for the Brown and White's big Rival.

(As documented in *Legends of Lehigh - Lafayette*, Brunner is the only player to ever score points for both Lehigh and Lafayette in the Rivalry.)

The twenty-two year old Brunner also benefitted greatly by Sutherland's recruitment of Frank "Dutch" Schwab, guard for Lafayette's 1921 team.

Schwab graduated from high school in 1912, and then worked in the anthracite coal mines until the Great War, where he served as an army sergeant. There he played for a service team, where he was seen by Sutherland and enrolled at Lafayette.

"Dutch" Schwab listed 1898 as his birth year, though that implies he graduated from high school at the age of 14. When he played at Lafayette, he was at the minimum a 23 year old sophomore, and most likely even older, perhaps as old as 27.

"Lafayette's foot-ball team never prays or weeps before a game," *The Pittsburgh Leader* wrote of the Maroon and White. "Those silly Maroons merely go in and wallop their rivals."

Frank "Dutch" Schwab

Lafayette bulldozed their way through their schedule, beating Bucknell 20-7, dominating Rutgers 35-0, defeating Fordham 28-7, crushing Penn 38-6, and humiliating Delaware 44-0. As anticipated, Lafayette would also dominate Lehigh by a similar score, 28-6.

All season, however, Lafayette had to continuously defend the presence of star players Brunner and Schwab, as well as other great athletes that ended up with careers in professional baseball. Back Mike Gazella would eventually have Babe Ruth as a teammate on the Yankees, while their freshman end, Charlie Berry, would have a pro career in both the early NFL (Pottsville Maroons) and Major League Baseball (Philadelphia A's, Boston Red Sox, and Chicago White Sox).

"If Penn State beats Pittsburgh on Thursday," *The New York American* reported, "it will have an equal right to share first [Eastern] honors with Lafayette, though Lafayette has a number of students who are bona fide students only in name. One of those players [Brunner] was at Pennsylvania last year, and there is no telling where he will be next season... Lafayette does not contribute to the good of the game by tolerating players who violate the spirit of the sport."

In a rebuttal posted in *The Lafayette*, Dean Heckel explained that Brunner was a bona fide student, being current in nine or more credit hours at the college. He also said that Brunner "was admitted to Lafayette last year with the proviso that he should not at any time represent the college on any of our athletic teams; this man, however, made an excellent record in scholarship and general behavior and on the basis of this – he having met our requirement of one year's residence – the Faculty re-considered his case."

Lafayette's 1921 Football Team ("Boots" Brunner, bottom row, 2nd from right)

Brunner stayed in school another year, in time to earn all-American honors for Lafayette the following season in 1922. Lafayette competed against big, national powers like Pittsburgh, Boston College, and Washington and Jefferson, battling to a 6-1 record.

Lehigh fought "heavier and more formidable" Lafayette that season to a 3-0 defeat, settled only after a late field goal by Brunner.

"Much has been written of the Lehigh University's wonderful fighting spirit in times of distress," *The New York Times* wrote in regards to the

Brown and White's tough, injury-riddled season, "yet it is doubtful if ever a team of the past made a stand like that of Coach Jim Baldwin's men here this afternoon in the face of overwhelming odds."

Stalemated at 0-0, and driving with 3 minutes to play on Lehigh's 16 yard line, "it was decided to stake all on a drop kick by 'Bots' Brunner," *The New York Times* continued. "He dropped back to the 27 yard line and then calmly booted the ball between the uprights for the only score of the game."

Little did Lehigh fans know that they would only score a field goal over the next five contests vs. Lafayette, getting outscored 112-3 by the Maroon and White over that stretch.

The Roaring Twenties, so named because of peacetime economic prosperity, was not roaring for the Brown and White.

In 1924, Lafayette decided to name their nationally-renowned football team the Leopards.

"The Leopard is to be the official mascot of the Lafayette football team," *The Lafayette* reported. "This was decided last night at the regular meeting of the Student Council held in Brainerd Hall. A Leopard skin has been ordered and will be worn by a student at the Penn and W. & J. games, and was met with approval."

The Leopard skin initially had a 1-1 record for Lafayette, it first being unveiled in front of 25,000 fans at the Polo Grounds in New York in a neutral-site contest against the Eastern powerhouse Washington and Jefferson. The Leopards beat the Presidents 20-6, but lost to Penn the following week, 6-3. (The Leopard skin may not have been needed for Lafayette to win their sixth straight game over Lehigh, a 7-0 victory.)

Lafayette's fame in the college football world went national. A set of football cards was issued in 1924 depicting the entire team.

Meanwhile in Bethlehem, many injuries - and one death - became the hallmark of this low point in Lehigh athletics.

In 1925, Brown and White team captain Charlie Prior was returning a punt against West Virginia Wesleyan, and was tackled badly, shattering the sixth vertebra in his back. He would be hospitalized from this injury, and die two weeks later.

Sympathy poured out from Lehigh's remaining opponents, which included powerful Georgetown. The sympathy did not do much to help Lehigh's competitiveness on the field, though. The "Hilltoppers," as Georgetown was then known, crushed the Brown and White 40-0.

Lehigh had Lafayette's sympathy for Prior's death as well, but also lost the game to their Rivals resoundingly, 14-0.

By 1926, the gap between Lafayette and Lehigh would never seem greater.

Led by hall-of-fame head coach Herb McCracken, the Leopards would go a perfect 8-0-0 and lay a claim to be one of the best teams in the East once again heading into the Rivalry. Lehigh, on the other hand, entered the contest after a disappointing 1-7-0 season.

While Lehigh was being shut out by St. John's and the Quantico Marines, Lafayette was making trips to Pitt to face off against former Lafayette head football coach "Jock" Sutherland, and winning.

"Jock" Sutherland left Lafayette after the 1923 season to take over the Pitt Panthers' head coaching vacancy made available by the retirement of legendary hall of fame head coach "Pop" Warner. Sutherland would continue his own hall-of-fame head coaching career with Pittsburgh.

Herb McCracken

McCracken's teams never lost to Pitt, going 3-0 against the coach he replaced.

"Another fighting Maroon eleven has cornered the Panther in its own lair and conquered it," *The Lafayette* said in 1926 after the Leopards won a hard-fought battle with the Panthers, 17-7. "For the third successive year, Lafayette has emerged to the fore in the sports world by defeating the University of Pittsburgh. With the score tied, with the loss of their leader, with the memory of two periods in which they were outplayed, McCracken's men brought victory by a whirlwind finish which has become almost traditional."

When the team returned, the student body looked around for a place to build a bonfire to celebrate the team, looking first at the brand-new, $500,000 stadium named after trustee Thomas Fisher, but quickly getting turned down. Eventually the students would be allowed to build the bonfire at March Field, where the football team used to play before the construction of their brand-new stadium.

As "Jock" Sutherland's teams focused on defense, Herb McCracken's teams used a powerful offense to overwhelm. By the time Lafayette was about to finish the season against Lehigh, their 68-0 drubbing of Susquehanna placed the Leopards as the top scoring team in the East, according to *The Lafayette*, with halfback Mike Wilson leading the way.

By the big weekend, Lafayette fans, looking for their eighth straight win against their Rivals, were trying to fight overconfidence.

"Sure we've a good team," *The Lafayette* said, warning that the Rivalry game was not just about the spectacle. "Ask Washington & Jefferson. Ask Pitt. Ask five or six other colleges. Unbeatable? Intercollegiate champions? Not by a long shot - not 'til we down Lehigh."

"Lehigh's a good team, too," they continued. "Don't laugh. Six defeats — or is it seven? That's no matter. What, pardon the truism, does anything matter when Lafayette and Lehigh play? McCracken's motto? 'Win every game as it comes.' [Lehigh head coach Percy] Wendell's? 'Win the Lafayette game!'"

Game at Fisher Field, 1926

Lafayette fans wouldn't need to worry about overconfidence, as the Leopards would crush Lehigh, 35-0, in their final game of the season and stake a legitimate claim to being the best team in the nation, outscoring their opponents 327-37.

"As the sun, transmuted by the haze of November, into a sphere of flaming orange," *The Lafayette* said, "sank in the Bushkill Valley on Saturday that cry, once a call of appeal, of hope, became an exultant Paean of victory on the lips of the followers of the Maroon. The Maroon battered down a fighting Bethlehem team to score a 35-0 triumph. Chill, northwestern blasts did not daunt the crowd of 17,000 who came to watch the sixtieth battle between Lafayette and her rival of rivals, Lehigh."

As Lafayette celebrated their eighth straight win against the Brown and White, Lehigh alumni were not taking the beatings in stride.

"A letter arrived in my mail a week or so ago," Walter Okeson reported in the *Lehigh Alumni Bulletin* of 1927, "asking that instead of writing articles about the football team I give a plain answer as to what is wrong with Lehigh football."

Okeson, the former football star, was the voice of Lehigh athletics at the time. As player, coach, vice president and member of Lehigh's board of trustees, he embodied Brown and White football, defining the athletics program for a generation.

"New scholastic standards wiped out a lot of players," he continued, also noting that a big proportion of the team was flunking out each year, which Dr. Richards had warned him must stop. "New eligibility rules erased others, cessation of financial inducements choked up a big channel of supply. The devotees of the old system maintained that it was impossible to get and keep football material without paying for it both with money and special scholastic favors. They further claimed the administration and faculty were against football and were trying to wipe it out."

Even with these new standards, Okeson dismissed those that claimed the administration was against football.

Austin Tate

"Equally good and better material can be secured each year if the advantages of Lehigh are brought home to the boys in the prep and high schools," he also said. "For poor boys we have scholarships available."

Though the 1927 season was a disaster for Lehigh, Okeson did see some promise with a strong freshman football team, who played very well and would soon be working their way into the varsity.

These freshmen, coached by a former Lehigh alumnus and former Bethlehem High School coach, Austin Tate, would be the beginning of Lehigh's turnaround.

1928 seemed to be more of the same for Lehigh's struggles on the field, though the Brown and White showed some promise with close wins over Muhlenberg, Widener, and St. John's at home. Against the rest of their schedule, however, Lehigh would only score three points, and with Lafayette beating Penn State 7-0 the week before, there was little reason for the casual observer to believe that the Brown and White would be able to score.

"It has been nine long years since the Brown and White has registered a victory over the Maroon," *The Brown and White* observed. "The last tally against Lafayette was a well-directed field goal by "Honey" Lewis in 1923. It has been seven years since the Brown and White has crossed the Maroon goal line. But this has made the team of 1928 all the more determined to go down in gridiron history as the team that put a stop to this reign of Lafayette supremacy."

Outmanned, Lehigh would fall behind 38-0 to powerful Lafayette, but would finally break their scoreless streak.

"With Lehigh in possession of the ball on her own 29 yard line, Bob Harris completed a pass to Sam Hall, Lehigh wingman on Lafayette's 32 yard line," *The Brown and White* describes, "and three plays later directed the ball into the very shadows of the Maroon goal where Bob Many, Lehigh basketball star playing the end position, leaped skyward to grab it out of the hands of three Lafayette men and jog five yards for the first touchdown scored against Lafayette since 1921."

Lehigh would tack on another touchdown to make the final tally 38-14, "the largest score piled up against Lafayette since the Armistice was signed in 1918," *The Brown and White* continued.

"Practically their entire cheering section moved on the field and celebrated," *The Lafayette* added, "more than the Lafayette fans who were watching their team roll up their tenth successive victory. Lafayette was scoring on every few plays and seemed to be on their way to surpass last year's one-sided score when Coach [Herb] McCracken started to use the reserves."

With the scoring drought finally over, one of the most thrilling Rivalry contests occurred in 1929.

Lafayette was having an off year. They entered the game 3-5, but still expected to beat their old Rival that they had regularly beaten for a decade. Lehigh was going in with a 3-3-2 record, but hopes were higher than they had been in some time.

The 1929 game started with the quarterback, Ed Davidowitz, leading

Lehigh to a game-opening touchdown, giving Lehigh their first lead over Lafayette since 1924, 7-0.

A few series later, he would connect with halfback Tom Nora, twenty yards downfield. Nora, eluding Lafayette's defensive back, ran thirty more yards to score another Lehigh touchdown.

They missed the extra point to go up 13-0, but Lafayette would roar back and get a touchdown of their own. The extra point, though, would be blocked by tackle Tubby Miller, making the score 13-6 as the clock ticked down to halftime.

The second half would be a series of thrilling defensive stops for Lehigh. Twice the Leopards got to Lehigh's goal line, and twice the Brown and White stopped them short of the goal. Lafayette's diminutive star halfback, Al Socolow, had to be taken off the field in a stretcher, but Lafayette still kept surging dangerously close to Lehigh's goal.

When Lafayette finally came through to score, "Cook, one of the most accurate placement kickers in the East," *The Brown and White* reported, "confidently stood on the ten yard line waiting to score the tying point. But half a dozen Lehigh linemen surged through and Tommy Ayre, who had replaced McLernon at center, just touched the ball with his fingers, deflecting it to the right and spoiling the kick as the Lehigh stands went wild."

Lehigh had to frantically hold on as the final quarter came to a close. One Lafayette drive came close, but an interception stopped it. With five minutes remaining, one Lafayette drive reached the goal. Cook would try a field goal that would give Lafayette the lead.

"The crowd of 18,000 was silent as Cook again casually made his preparations," the students reported. "The ball was snapped. Cook stepped forward and kicked. No Lehigh player was close enough to block the ball, but the Lafayette tackle was so hurried that his kick went wild to the right of the goalposts."

Lehigh would withstand the constant Lafayette pressure, and break the streak by the narrowest of margins, 13-12.

After the game, the band stormed the field, as did thousands of Lehigh supporters. The Packer Hall bell, silent since the Armistice, the last time Lehigh beat Lafayette in Bethlehem, finally rung out on the Lehigh campus to symbolize a Lehigh victory over their old Rival.

"It's been done! It's been done!" *The Brown and White* exclaimed in their recap. "For three days bonfires, cheers, paint, and wild celebrations have proclaimed this fact; but Lehigh students are still trying to make themselves believe that it is true, that after 11 years of expectant hopes and bitter disappointments their football team finally triumphed over the Lafayette Leopard."

This win in the Rivalry was the turning point.

No more would the expectation be for Lehigh to merely score against their Rivals, who were still competing for national honors. It was a game that was competitive once again. The win would spur the Rivalry forward when it was on the brink of being cancelled.

The Rivalry has endured twists and turns, through the evolution of the sport, through shared history, through scandals, through a World War and through Lafayette's dominance on the field for long stretches. Through everything, a strong bond was forged between the two schools which continues today. No other college football rivalry can compete with Lehigh and Lafayette's Rivalry in terms of history, circumstance, and number of games played.

BIBLIOGRAPHY

Condit, Uzal W., **The History of Easton: 1739-1885**, George West, Publisher, 1885

Davidson, Todd and Donchez, Bob, **Legends of Lehigh – Lafayette: College Football's Most-Played Rivalry**, Bethlehem, PA, D&D Publishing, 1997

Davis, Parke H., **Football: The American Intercollegiate Game**, New York, NY, Scribner Press, 1911

Edwards, William M., **Memories of the Game and the Men Behind the Ball**, New York, NY, Moffett Yard and Company, 1916

Gendebein, Albert W., **Friedrich List and Lafayette College**, University Park, PA, Penn State University Press, 1962

Gendebein, Albert W., **Science the Handmaiden of Religion: The Origins of the Pardee Scientific Course at Lafayette College**, University Park, PA, Penn State University Press, 1966

Henry, M. S., **History of the Lehigh Valley**, Easton, PA, Bixler & Corwin, 1860

Hughes, Thomas, **Tom Brown's School Days**, Cambridge, PA, MacMillian, 1857

Kieffer, Henry M., **Some of the First Settlers Of the Forks of the Delaware and their Descendants**, Lancaster, PA, New Era Printing Company, 1902

Klosk, Edwin. G. Mgr, **Twenty Year Book of the Lehigh University**, South Bethlehem, PA, Lehigh University, 1886

Lehigh Valley Historical Society, **Proceedings and Papers Read Before the Lehigh Valley Historical Society**, Allentown, PA, 1921

March, Francis A. Jr., **Athletics at Lafayette College**, Easton, PA, Cornell Publications Printing, 1926

Reichel, William C., **A History of the Moravian Seminary for Young Ladies**, Fourth Edition, Lancaster, PA, New Era Printing Company, 1901

Skillman, David B., **The Biography of a College: Lafayette**, Volumes I and II, New York, NY, Scribner Press, 1932

Smith, Courtney M., **A Delicate Balance: An Examination of Lehigh University's Athletic Culture and Athletic Extra-Curriculum, 1866-1998**, Ann Arbor, MI, UMI Dissertation Publishing, 2009

Smith, Ronald A., **Pay for Play: A History of Big-Time College Athletic Reform**, Champaign, IL, University of Illinois Press, 2001

Treese, Lorett, **Railroads of New Jersey: Fragments of the Past in the Garden State Landscape**, Mechanicsburg, PA, Stackpole Books, 2006

Yates, W. Ross, **Lehigh University: A History of Education in Engineering, Business, and the Human Condition**, Bethlehem, PA, Lehigh University Press, 1992

Primary Newspaper Archive Sources

The Allentown Morning Call, Allentown, PA
The Bethlehem Globe-Times, Bethlehem, PA
The Brown and White, Bethlehem, PA
The Easton Express-Times, Easton, PA
Harper's Weekly
The Lafayette, Easton, PA
The Lehigh Alumni Bulletin, Bethlehem, PA
Lehigh Epitome Yearbooks, Bethlehem, PA
The Lehigh Quarterly, Bethlehem, PA
The New York Times, New York, NY

Digital Resources

Delaware Water Gap NRA Historic Resource Study
The Internet Archive
LA 84 Foundation Digital Research Online
The Library of Congress
SULAIR Copyright Renewal Database
Wikimedia Commons

ABOUT THE AUTHOR

Chuck Burton attended his first Rivalry game in 1988 as a Lehigh University undergraduate. In 2001, he became the founder and head writer of *Lehigh Football Nation*, an influential website chronicling Lehigh University's football program. Burton has also written extensively about FCS football for media outlets including *The College Sports Journal*.

In 2014 he attended his 25th Lehigh/Lafayette football game. That year marked the 150th meeting of Lehigh and Lafayette, which took place at Yankee Stadium in New York.

CPSIA information can be obtained
at www.ICGtesting.com
Printed in the USA
BVOW08s1119201217

503315BV00020B/1790/P